EXTRA STUFF

Gambling Ramblings

by Peter Griffin

Huntington Press
Las Vegas, Nevada

Published by Huntington Press
P.O. Box 28041, Las Vegas, Nev. 89126
(Tel: 702-871-4363)

First Edition

ISBN 0-929712-00

For Lydia and Kurt,
my friends and gambling associates.

EXTRA STUFF

CONTENTS

ACKNOWLEDGMENTS ix

FOREWORD by Anthony Curtis xi

1 **A MATHEMATICIAN LOOKS AT CRAPS PROBABILI-TIES, EXPECTATIONS, AND BETTING SYSTEMS** 1
Chances of Winning at Craps 2
Negative Expectation at the Crap Table 6
A Gambling System 7

2 **GRIFFIN ON BLACKJACK** 13
Casino Attitudes Toward Counters Changing He
  Thinks 15
'Bonanza' on Early Surrender? 16

3 **HOW LONG MUST WE WAIT FOR AN IMPROBABLE EVENT TO OCCUR?**
An Old Gambler's Rule of Thumb 19
Some Examples 22
Natural Log of Two 23
Of Means and Medians 24
Birthdays in the Next Issue 26

4 **MEANS AND MEDIANS OF WAITING DISTRIBUTIONS** 27
How Many People to Get All Birthdays? 29
But How Can We Find the Median? 31
Next Time More Birthdays 34

5 MATCHING BIRTHDAZE 37
At Least Two Matching Days 38
Three or More People on the Same Day 40

6 A PARADOXICAL PROPOSITION 43
A Build Up of Consecutive Sevens 45
The Long Run 46
Who Will Win Next? 47
Other Strangeness 48

**7 SHOULD YOU GAMBLE IF THEY GIVE BACK
HALF YOUR LOSSES?** 49

8 AN ALL-TIME HIGH — HOW OFTEN? 59
Random Walk 59
One Dimensional Random Walk as a Model for
  Gambling Problems 62
Chance of Being at an All-Time High 64
Next Time Games With Variable Payoffs 67

**9 GAMBLER'S RUIN FORMULAS FOR NON-UNIT
PAYOFFS** 69
Chance of Ruin Before Doubling Fortune 70
Approximating Gambler's Ruin Formulas in
  Other Cases 73
Games With More Than Two Possible Outcomes 77

10 OPTIMAL WAGERS ON SIMULTANEOUS BETS 85

11 TRANSCENDENTAL PROBABILITIES 93

**12 DIFFERENT WAYS TO DESCRIBE WIN RATE
(OR PC)** 107
Hold Percentage 107
Throwing Out Ties 110
Disagreements on Blackjack Percentage 111
Uston vs. ECON 113
My Craps System With an Average Win Rate
  of 56% 115

**13 DISCONTINUITY AT THE GOLDEN MEAN
(A paradox of proportional betting)** 119
Golden Mean 125

**14 SELF-STYLED EXPERTS TAKE A BATH
IN RENO** 129

**15 MATHEMATICAL EXPECTATION FOR THE PUBLIC'S
PLAY IN CASINO BLACKJACK** 135
   I   Introduction 136
   II   Other Studies 137
   III Basic Strategy, Definition and Implication for
       Casinos 139
   IV How I Did It 140
   V   How Well Does the Public Play Blackjack? 143
   VI Possible Objections 150
   VII Per Capita and Per Dollar Win Rates 152
   Acknowledgements 156
   References 156

16 EXTRA STUFF 157
   Peter Griffin's Blackjack Quiz 157
      Answers 158
   A Typical Book Review 160
   Griffin Comments on 8-Spot Keno Ticket Story 161
   Guru Goof? 162
   So You Think You Know Craps by S.N. Ethier 164
      Craps Quiz 165
      Solutions to Problems 1-3 167
   April 1, 1983, Las Vegas 169

INDEX 171

Acknowledgments

Thanks to: Karen Hunt for the cover design and back cover photo; the Four Queens' Dick LeVasseur, Lynn Sullivan and Mike Moore for allowing us to invade their casino for our photo shoot; Huntington Press' Lori Fahning Thompson for her work in the book's early stages and for her formidable (in some instances uncanny) proofreading exploits; John Speer and Don Schlesinger for punctuation errors they will find; Howard Schwartz and Edna Luckman for permission to reproduce the *Casino & Sports* articles; Stewart Ethier for permission to include his craps quiz; a special thanks to Bethany Coffey, Huntington Press' bright talent, for her contributions in typesetting, page layout, editing, and all other aspects of this book's physical existence.

Also: Addie Wright and Jack Christopher for looking after the animals; also to Jack for computer help over the years; Blair Rodman for helping to open the champagne; Mr. Pele and Sue for being who they were; Eleanor Alexander, my high school Latin teacher, for instruction superior to any other I experienced in my scholastic career; my parents for seeing to it that I grew up in a house filled with books; and John Luckman, who continues to look after us all.

Foreword
by Anthony Curtis

I came to Las Vegas in 1979 with a clearly defined, two-part plan: first, become a successful blackjack card counter; then, parlay gambling knowledge and winnings into a successful publishing career. Little did I know that the author of a book being published that same year would play a key role in both parts of my plan. The book was *The Theory of Blackjack*. The author was Peter Griffin.

The Theory of Blackjack became my bible and Griffin became my unknowing mentor. I read and reread his book; collected his gambling conference papers; and, waited eagerly for each new edition of *Casino & Sports*, a respected, albeit lightly-read periodical to which Peter contributed an assortment of articles. Those *C&S* articles were classics. Unfortunately, the magazine's readership wasn't large enough to justify costs and effort. *Casino & Sports* ceased publishing in the early eighties.

With the exception of a gambling conference paper every few years and an occasional letter published in the newsletters of Stanford Wong or Arnold Snyder, Peter wrote little that was seen by the general public following *C&S's* demise. He chose not to rehash old subjects in any of the new gambling publications that were popping up and disappearing with regularity. The result was aptly described by Howard Schwartz (former editor of the *C&S* series): "A whole decade [of players] has lost touch with Peter Griffin."

Due to happenstance, luck, a favorable deviation — call it what you like — I became friends with Peter in 1982. On occasion we would discuss the *C&S* articles. I wanted to assemble them in book form. Peter declined: "It's all been said before. This is just *extra stuff.*"

It took a few years, but I eventually wore him down. The result is the collection of new and improved, expanded, amended and updated articles from *C&S* that is contained within. A selection of *stuff* from other sources — periodicals, personal correspondence, a major gambling conference — has been incorporated to complete the effort. The chapters are arranged, for the most part, in the chronological order in which they were written.

In keeping with the prevailing attitude of the nineties, I assume that the reader is at this point asking, "What's in it for me?" The experienced gambler can expect to encounter ideas and concepts that he has not considered in the past. This applies to devotees of all the games. Sports bettors, for example, will find a wealth of information on proportional and simultaneous wagering. The beginning gambler will come away understanding the injurious implications of playing negative expectation games, and recognizing the folly of trying to beat them with money management or progressive betting systems. Casino personnel will benefit from a discussion on how to properly evaluate "win rates" and "hold percentages." For the casino executive in a decision making capacity, I firmly believe that Peter's analysis of the *Mathematical Expectation for the Public's Play in Casino Blackjack* (Chapter 15) is one of the most pertinent and useful gambling studies ever done! The greatest rewards will be realized by serious students of gambling, and those who aspire to profit from opportunities that arise in the gambling world. While this book does not contain the keys to the kingdom, it does supply weaponry that will enhance your arsenal.

Howard Schwartz, commenting further on Peter's stature in the gambling industry said, "When Griffin talks, people listen." There is no disputing this. A whole new generation of gambling enthusiasts now has an opportunity to listen...and learn. As for me, I'm writing the Foreword to a book written by one of my heroes. How many people get to do something like that?

1

A MATHEMATICIAN LOOKS AT CRAPS PROBABILITIES, EXPECTATIONS, AND BETTING SYSTEMS

As you read this article you will become aware of why numerologists regard this year as being a significant one for dice players: 1980 is the least common denominator for the craps probabilities!

If you enjoy the pastime of shooting crap, well and good. My purpose in writing this article is not to reform you, but, rather, to communicate the mathematician's perspective—why he regards any "expert advice on how to bet at craps" as being equivalent to expert advice on "how to smoke cigarettes" or "how to be run over by a cement truck."

(Within a few years of writing this article I made the acquaintance of "Sal" from Brooklyn and had to recant this opinion. Sal could control one die, either by sliding it or putting an inordinate amount of spin on it. I witnessed an audition at Lake Tahoe: at a given signal Sal's confederate slipped a $500 bet on the "field". Sal tossed a controlled six, another six occurred by chance, and the confederate won $1500. As he absconded with the winnings he was almost

tackled by the pit boss, offering him a comp to the restaurant!

Another time Sal was playing alone for low stakes at the now demolished Silver Slipper. When his "hard six on the hop" bet for $15 was ruled "no action" by the pit boss (Sal hit it; needless to say) he got angry. He went to make a phone call, returning to mumble "The cavalry is coming". Minutes later his confederate arrived, subsequently winning a $500 field bet when Sal had the dice.

The last time I saw Sal, shortly before his untimely departure from this mortal coil, he was working on controlling both dice—Sal didn't like the insecurity of only a 67% edge!)

We'll divide the discussion into three parts: First, how is the player's chance of winning at craps calculated; second, what is **expectation**, and in particular; what is this **negative expectation** associated with all of the independent trials casino gambles; and last, why are "money management" betting schemes doomed to ultimate failure in games like craps?

Chances of Winning at Craps

There are 36 equally likely ways for a pair of dice to land. This fact has occasionally been obscured because of the practically identical appearance of the two dice used in most games. Indeed, it is suggested that the famous mathematician Leibnitz believed there were only 21 possibilities because, for example, he thought of the total of 11 = 6 + 5 as being only one possibility, equiprobable with 12 = 6 + 6.

The best way to convince ourselves of the thirtysixness of it all is to imagine that the two dice are of different colors, say, one red and one green. The following display pictures all 36 possibilities, if we agree that the left most number in a parenthetical pair corresponds to the number of spots on the red die's uppermost face and the rightmost number is the result for the green die. Red six and green five, designated by (65) is different, then, from red five and green six, symbolized by (56).

(11) (12) (13) (14) (15) (16)
(21) (22) (23) (24) (25) (26)
(31) (32) (33) (34) (35) (36)
(41) (42) (43) (44) (45) (46)
(51) (52) (53) (54) (55) (56)
(61) (62) (63) (64) (65) (66)

The player's chance, or probability, of winning on the initial roll of the dice by throwing a total of eleven ("Yoeleven," I believe it is announced) is therefore the fraction 2/36, representing the two ways to roll eleven out of the 36 possibilities. Similarly, since there are six ways to make a total of seven,

the chance of winning on the first toss with a seven is 6/36.

The shooter may also lose immediately on the come out roll, 4/36 of the time when he throws (11), (12), (21), or (66). The difficulty in calculating the player's probability of winning at craps occurs when he "establishes his point" and must roll again.

Let's imagine the player rolls an initial total of nine. At this stage he has neither won nor lost; both results are still possible, but we want to measure, conditionally, how probable it is that he will now win. He must continue to roll the dice until he achieves either seven or nine, so we blot the other totals out of the chart since they affect only the duration of the game, but not the result.

					(16)
				(25)	
			(34)		(36)
		(43)		(45)	
	(52)		(54)		
(61)		(63)			

We see that of the ten possible terminating rolls above, four are winners and six are losers. Hence 4/10 is the conditional chance of winning if the player's point is nine. The overall chance of winning by first throwing a nine and then making the point before "sevening out" is formed by multiplying 4/36 (the chance of an initial throw of nine) and 4/10.

Now the following table of possibilities and probabilities for the player winning at craps can be created:

Initial Total	Chance of Total	Chance of winning with this total	Chance of this total and winning with it
4	3/36	3/9	$3/36 \times 3/9 = 55/1980$
5	4/36	4/10	$4/36 \times 4/10 = 88/1980$
6	5/36	5/11	$5/36 \times 5/11 = 125/1980$
7	6/36	—	$6/36 = 330/1980$
8	5/36	5/11	$5/36 \times 5/11 = 125/1980$
9	4/36	4/10	$4/36 \times 4/10 = 88/1980$
10	3/36	3/9	$3/36 \times 3/9 = 55/1980$
11	2/36	—	$2/36 = \underline{110/1980}$
		Total Chance of Winning	$= 976/1980$

Because the probability of winning is 976/1980 (found by adding the figures in the last column, expressed with a common denominator of 1980 for convenience), the chance of losing must be (1980 − 976)/1980 = 1004/1980, since these two fractions must add up to one. Skeptics (or pessimists) can make a similar table of probabilities and possibilities for the player losing to verify this.

What about the "don't pass bar (66)" bettor? How often will he win? We know he loses as often as the "pass" bettor wins, 976/1980 of the time, but he doesn't necessarily win in the other 1004 cases that the "pass" bettor loses. The outcome (66) is a standoff for the "don't" bettor, and this occurs 1/36, or 55/1980, of the time. Hence the "don't" bettor, loses 976/1980, ties 55/1980, and wins 949/1980 of the time so that the resultant fractions total one.

5

Negative Expectation at the Crap Table!

The player's "expectation" is defined as the sum of all possible changes in the player's fortune, multiplied by their associated probabilities before summing. For the "pass line" bet the expectation is

$$+1 \times 976/1980 - 1 \times 1004/1980 = -28/1980$$

and for the "don't" bet we have

$$+1 \times 949/1980 - 1 \times 976/1980 = -27/1980.$$

These figures are often quoted as percentages of −1.41% and −1.36% per play for the "pass" and "don't pass" bettors respectively. To a mathematician the "don't pass" is slightly preferable, but neither bet is desirable because of the negative sign preceding each **average result** ("expectation" can be thought of as synonymous with this term).

There is another way to look at the "don't" bet if we assume the bettor is determined to leave the bet out if (66) is rolled. With this interpretation the "don't" bet will win 949 times out of 949 + 976 = 1925 decided cases. Thus, if we ignore ties, the "don't" bettor's chance of winning is 949/1925 = .492987, startlingly close to the "do" bettor's 976/1980 = .492929. The "don't" bet expectation can be regarded, in this formulation, as (949 − 976)/1925 = −1.40% unit *per resolved bet*.

It is known that if the game of craps is played often enough these average results of −1.41% and −1.36% will be virtually exactly realized by the

6

"pass" and "don't pass" bettors. Think of the negative sign as a warning that continuing to play the game will be hazardous to your wealth; you will inexorably drift deeper into debt with only occasional spasmodic lurches toward solvency.

A Gambling System

A recently published craps system suggested that the player bet $2 on the pass line, let it ride if the bet won, and thereafter bet on the result which occurred time before last ("avant dernier" as the French say). So long as the player wins he increases his bet from two to four to five to nine to eleven, leveling the bet off at eleven even if the winning streak exceeds five (to avoid alerting the casino to the fact that it's facing a 'system' dice player?). After a loss the player reverts to the $2 wager.

The argument for switching from the "do" to the "don't" or vice versa, depending upon what happened the time before last, involves some irrelevant discourse about whether results will be 'choppy' or not. This sort of extraneous embellishment and overcomplication is typical of such systematizing, having the purpose, one suspects, of obscuring the fundamental futility of the enterprise.

Epstein (*The Theory of Gambling and Statistical Logic*) writes on p. 56 "No advantage accrues to betting only on some subsequence of a number of independent trials." We might equally well switch tables or switch casinos, rather than switching bets, for all the difference it will make. As we saw in the last section the "don't" bet gives us a slightly better chance of winning, but for all practical purposes both bets can be assumed to have the same chance of winning, .493, and the doctrine of independence assures us we can find no guidance in "the result before the last one." Epstein (p. 53): "Betting systems constitute one of the oldest delusions of gambling history . . . votaries are spiritually akin to the proponents of perpetual motion machines, butting their heads against the second law of thermodynamics."

So much for the business of switching from the pass line to the "don't" bet; now let's deal with the sacred selection of 2, 4, 5, 9, 11, ...11 as being the appropriate amount to bet in the midst of a winning streak. Epstein again (p. 53): "Any and all betting systems lead ultimately to the *same* value of mathematical expectation of gain per unit amount wagered." We shall illustrate this, first with theoretical probability and then by playing several hundred thousand games of craps using this betting system.

Suppose we agree that a "sequence of bets" means those bets up to and including a loss, a new sequence beginning after the previous loss. The length of a sequence is variable; we can have a short sequence of only one bet if we lose it. In such a case we put a total of $2 into action and lost a net of $2. This will happen with a probability of .507, since we're agreed that either the "do" or the "don't" bet have .493 probability of winning, to three digits.

A longer sequence might be 2, 4, 5, and 9, with the underlining denoting that the bet was lost.

Here we put $20 into action and won a net of $2. The chance of this occurring is .493 × .493 × .493 × .507 = .06075. A table of the possible sequences, the action per sequence, net gain or loss, and probability of the sequence occurring follows:

Number of Wins in Sequence	Total Action for Sequence	Net Profit or Loss (–)	Chance of Sequence
0	2	–2	.507
1	6	–2	.24995
2	11	1	.12323
3	20	2	.06075
4	31	9	.02995
5	42	20	.01477
6	53	31	.00728
7	64	42	.00359
8	75	53	.00177
9	86	64	.00087
10	97	75	.00043
11	108	86	.00021
12	119	97	.00010
13	130	108	.00005

Of course, the table can be extended, but observe that, in this case, the profitable sequences are the ones with the smallest probabilities. The ultimate imbalance of profit and loss, achieved by multiplying appropriate probabilities, is what dooms any and all such "money management" schemes whenever there is the intention to continue to play.

If we multiply the second column "action" per sequence times the fourth column probability and total up (mathematicians have ways of adding up an infinite number of such quantities) we discover that the average action per sequence is $7.547. Doing the same multiplication and summing for the third and fourth columns we find the average net loss to be $ −.106. Dividing −.106 by 7.547 produces our old friend −1.4% and thus illustrates Epstein's last quoted remark!

The next table empirically verifies the previous theory, being the result of two separate computer simulations of 100,000 such sequences.

Number of Wins in Sequence	First Simulation	Second Simulation
0	50652	50542
1	25129	25167
2	12425	12223
3	6038	6168
4	2900	2990
5	1489	1474
6	682	747
7	307	338
8	186	181
9	95	89
10	51	41
11	26	22
12	13	10
13	3	2
14	2	3
15	1	3
19	1	0
Total Action	750187	755631
Net Result	−13019	−10927
% Return	−1.73%	−1.45%

Now it's true that there are some betting schemes which can give the player a high probability of a small win. A famous example of this is the "doubling up" system, wherein we double our bet after a loss. Suppose, for instance, we're trapped in Las Vegas with $511. An airline ticket home costs $512 and the crap tables are open to provide us the opportunity to win the extra dollar.

Doubling up after a loss will enable us to gain the extra dollar unless we lose nine times in a row. This latter event is improbable, occurring about .002214 of the time, but the loss in this case is catastrophic, $511. We win our extra dollar the other .997786 of the time, and the arithmetic, $1 \times (.997786) - 511 \times (.002214) = -.1335$, leaves us again with a negative expectation for the effort. Had we the patience we'd discover our average action per sequence was just under $10, yielding again the -1.4% expectation per unit bet.

Despite the fact that it was proven almost two centuries ago that one couldn't trisect an angle with ruler and compass alone, mathematicians are continually presented with new 'proofs' that it is indeed possible. So, if you come up with a new betting scheme, keep it to yourself.

Do like Chris Evert in the Wilson tennis racquet ad: "I *play* with it and I *win* with it!"

Author & Editor- *Peter clowns with Howard Schwartz at* The Gambler's Book Club. *Howard edited* Casino & Sports, *the magazine in which several of this book's essays originally appeared.*

2

GRIFFIN ON BLACKJACK

Editor's Note: Some of the world's greatest gambling theorists, wits and intellectuals stop in at the GBC (Gambler's Book Club) unexpectedly. Recently, Peter Griffin, author of The Theory of Blackjack, *published by GBC late in 1979 [now published by Huntington Press], made an unexpected foray into Las Vegas, visiting with us. Griffin happens to have all three qualities — much theory plus an ample supply of both wit and intellect. What follows is Griffin's opinion and his reactions to questions we at* Casino & Sports *initiated and some remarks he offered spontaneously.*

Can an exact blackjack "machine" (computer program) be built to determine the precise basic strategy for any number of decks and any number of rules? Griffin, says he's working on one — and calls it "his first love."

"What's unique about this, is that I now have a procedure for calculating absolutely accurate pair-splitting expectations when repeated pair-splitting is used, as it is in almost all versions of casino blackjack. There have been some startling findings in the basic strategies, both single and multiple deck. Dealer hits soft-17, dealer stands on soft-17. Double after split, no-double after split. I'm really anxious to communicate these to the blackjack public."

Griffin has gotten favorable reaction from his theory book and says many players "have had their eyes opened to various aspects of blackjack which they had never imagined to be important before." He says many readers' "perspectives have been greatly enlarged — for example, they realize now the point-count systems are not in themselves infallible determiners of strategy — they are merely approximations. This is one of the points I tried to make in the book."

In looking to the future, he disagrees with some experts who predict casinos will move to an "infinite deck" for the obvious goal of fewer winners, less troubles with counters.

Griffin explains the term: "If we can imagine the number of decks being used not being four or six, but more, increasing the number continually, until, for instance, we might imagine using all the cards right now in Las Vegas — hundreds of thousands of decks all shuffled together, then card-counting would be futile at best. The removal of a particular card would have almost no effect at all on the probabilities for subsequently drawn cards. For example: let's assume we have 100,000 decks of cards all mixed together and you draw three fives. You now have 15 and you're thinking of whether to draw again. In single deck blackjack, if you have three fives, your chance of drawing another five is almost one fourth of what it would normally be, because there's only one five left in the deck. Whereas in the 100,000-deck games, there would be only a minuscule decrease in your chance of drawing another five."

Casino Attitudes Toward Counters
Changing He Thinks

He does not see casinos going to more than a six-deck shoe — the maximum he's seen used anywhere. [He was wrong: In Atlantic City they use eight.] It is Griffin's personal opinion casinos now realize they are not losing "enormous amounts" to card counters.

"They [the casinos] may be losing money to various forms of cheating, peeking, hole card, that sort of thing. I think the casinos have changed their attitude a little bit — maybe it doesn't show on the tables, but quite a few people highly placed in casino management that I know [who "comp" him to a meal here and there], recognize that card counting itself cannot really bankrupt a casino in any short period of time. And for any card-counter who's competent, there are ten who aren't really competent, and not only that, but there are thousands of people who are pouring money over the tables at a rate that not even the best card counters could compensate for on a one to one basis."

He thinks "counters create more interest in gambling and in the game of blackjack itself. I think the casinos are starting to reach a sort of equilibrium point with respect to how many decks they are willing to deal and where they shuffle the deck."

"Casinos previously thought counters could work some sort of magic with the odds — maybe get five or six per cent edge on them and this is not the case — if they can get a couple of per cent they're really very lucky. The average, typical, player is playing, I'd say, at a three per cent disadvantage."

One of the funniest moves Griffin has ever observed in blackjack casino play was perpetrated by a man who stood on two threes. "I watched him debate a long time whether or not to split threes against a six. And he thought better of it so he stood, taking no other card."

'Bonanza' On Early Surrender?

Griffin commented on New Jersey's rules on "early surrender": "The player in New Jersey gets a bit of a bonanza there on early surrender, where the player facing a bad hand against a dealer's ace showing, for instance, gets to duck out of the hand for half price before the dealer even looks and possibly has a blackjack. And 30 per cent of the time, the dealer's going to beat him anyway without him agonizing whether he's going to bust or not."

"The early surrender option gives the player about 6/10ths of one per cent which he might not ordinarily have." As a player, Griffin says he'd like to see this in Nevada too — "I'd also like to see all casinos stand on soft 17 and let me double after split and deal all 52 cards of a single deck — but I don't expect this. There are many things which I'd like but which I don't feel entitled to, nor do I expect Santa Claus to come down the chimney with them."

Speaking of Improbable Events - *Peter and Lydia Griffin: met September 1977; married Saturday, August 12, 1989.*

3

HOW LONG MUST WE WAIT FOR AN IMPROBABLE EVENT TO OCCUR?

An Old Gambler's Rule of Thumb

A classical probability problem is the one ascribed to the Chevalier de Mere in the mid-17th century (but actually posed and answered incorrectly by the Italian, Cardano, a century earlier):

How many rolls of a pair of dice make it more likely than not that a pair of sixes will have been cast?

To solve this problem exactly, a back door technique is useful. We instead calculate the probability that a pair of sixes will not have been thrown as the number of tosses increases, and wait until this probability dips below 1/2 for the first time. The chance of tossing a pair of sixes is 1/36 so the chance of not getting this event on a particular roll is $1 - 1/36 = 35/36$. You may use your calculator, if you have one, to show that the chance of 24 consecutive rolls without a pair of sixes is:

$$\underbrace{\frac{35}{36} \times \frac{35}{36} \times \ldots \times \frac{35}{36}}_{24 \text{ factors}} = \left(\frac{35}{36}\right)^{24} = .5086$$

19

Hence, the chance of at least one pair of sixes in the first 24 rolls is 1 − .5086 = .4914, which is still less than 1/2. One more multiplication gives:

$$\frac{35}{36} \times \frac{35}{36} \times \cdots \cdots \times \frac{35}{36} = \left(\frac{35}{36}\right)^{25} = .4945$$

$$\underbrace{\qquad\qquad\qquad\qquad}_{25 \text{ factors}}$$

and we realize that 25 rolls of the dice are necessary to have at least an even chance, the probability in this case being 1 − .4945 = .5055 of achieving at least one pair of sixes within the 25 tosses.

Somebody who knew "logarithms" could have found the answer more quickly by solving the following equation in which x is the unknown number of tosses necessary to have precisely an even chance:

$$\left(\frac{35}{36}\right)^{x} = \frac{1}{2}$$

$$x \ln \left(\frac{35}{36}\right) = - \ln 2$$

$$x = \frac{\ln 2}{\ln 36 - \ln 35} = \frac{.693}{3.583 - 3.555} = 24.6$$

Don't be troubled if you don't understand the manipulations or the symbol "ln" which stands for "natural logarithm." If you have a calculator with a natural log function you will be able to confirm these figures. The implication of these calculations is that 24 tosses is too few and 25 too many to have exactly an even chance. This is, of course, what we found by repeated multiplication.

A good mathematician could have come up with this result without a calculator or a set of log tables. He would have used an approximation to

$$\ln\left(\frac{35}{36}\right) = \ln\left(1 - \frac{1}{36}\right).$$

It is proven in calculus that $\ln(1 - y)$ is very close to $-y$, provided y is close to zero. If we apply this result to our equation

$$x \ln\left(\frac{35}{36}\right) = -\ln 2 \text{ or } x = \frac{-\ln 2}{\ln\left(\frac{35}{36}\right)},$$

we come up with

$$x = \frac{-\ln 2}{-y} = \frac{\ln 2}{y} = \frac{\ln 2}{\frac{1}{36}} = 36 \times \ln 2 = 36 \times .693 = 24.95$$

and reach the same conclusion as previously. What we did was approximate the value of

$$\ln\left(1 - \frac{1}{36}\right) \text{ with } -y = -\frac{1}{36}.$$

This, then, is what leads to the Gambler's Rule of Thumb: The number of trials necessary to have an even chance that a low probability event will occur is approximately .69 divided by that low probability.

Some Examples

Let's try a few more examples of the Rule. How many trials do we need to have about an even chance of tossing a total of eleven with two dice? Here the low probability event is "getting a total of eleven," which occurs 2/36 = 1/18 of the time. Our Gambler's Rule gives

$$\frac{.69}{\frac{1}{18}} = 18 \times .69 = 12.4,$$

which is accurate and much quicker than multiplying out

$$\left(\frac{17}{18}\right)^{12} = .5036 \text{ and } \left(\frac{17}{18}\right)^{13} = .4757,$$

then subtracting:

1 – .5036 = .4964 = chance of getting eleven in 12 tosses
1 – .4757 = .5243 = chance of getting eleven in 13 tosses.

The Rule, of course, is not infallible. If we used it to determine how many rolls of a single die would be required to have a better than even chance of rolling a four, we'd get 6 × .69 = 4.1 and assume four rolls wouldn't be enough when actually

$$\left(\frac{5}{6}\right)^4 = \frac{625}{1296}$$

is less than 1/2 so four rolls would give us a

$$1 - \frac{625}{1296} = \frac{671}{1296} = .518$$

chance of success. The problem here is that the

tossing of a four on a single die is not sufficiently improbable; 1/6 is too large.

Natural Log of Two

You probably realize that the .69 of our formula is a truncation of ln 2 = .693147. Here are three other ways for you to calculate this number more accurately.

1. Continue this series until you are exhausted:

$$1 - \tfrac{1}{2} + \tfrac{1}{3} - \tfrac{1}{4} + \tfrac{1}{5} - \tfrac{1}{6} + \tfrac{1}{7} - \tfrac{1}{8} + \tfrac{1}{9} - \text{etc.}$$

2. This is quicker:

$$\left(\tfrac{1}{2}\right)^1 + \tfrac{1}{2}\left(\tfrac{1}{2}\right)^2 + \tfrac{1}{3}\left(\tfrac{1}{2}\right)^3 + \tfrac{1}{4}\left(\tfrac{1}{2}\right)^4 + \tfrac{1}{5}\left(\tfrac{1}{2}\right)^5 + \dots \text{etc.}$$

3. Draw the hyperbola $y = \dfrac{1}{x}$

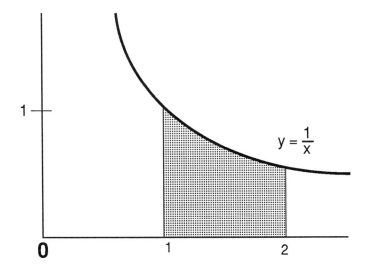

$$y = \frac{1}{x}$$

The shaded area under the graph of y = 1/x and between x = 1 and x = 2 is exactly ln 2 = .693147.

Isn't it wondrous that this mystical number plays such a role in geometry and probability at the same time?

Of Means and Medians

Now that you know that 25 tosses of the dice give you a better than even shot at producing a pair of sixes, would you want to accept the following proposition bet? I give you $30 to toss the dice until the first pair of sixes appears. You will then give me as many dollars as you required throws of the dice to produce that first pair of sixes. If it takes you twenty rolls you give me $20 and are a net $10 winner; if twenty-five rolls, you pay me $25 and net $5; if it takes thirty tosses we break even.

If your impulse is to accept the proposition you probably need a little lesson on the distinction between **means** and **medians,** two often different and often confused statistical measures of the middle of the distribution. It's true that you would win at least $5 at least half the time because 25 is the *median* of the distribution of the number of tosses necessary to terminate the game; the median is the smallest number such that at least 50% of the values of the distribution are less than or equal to it.

However, if we continued to play the game long enough you'd discover that I was winning an average net of $6 from you, even though you won more encounters than I did. (You'd win about 55%, we'd tie 1%, and I'd win 44%.) By now you begin to see what's happening: you can win at most $29, if you roll the twelve on the first toss. However, I could win, albeit improbably, a virtually limitless amount in any contest. In fact there's better than a 6% chance that you would need at least 100 tosses and hence that I would win at least $70.

How do I know so glibly that I would average $6 in winnings in the long run? Because I know that 36 is the *mean* of the distribution of tosses necessary. If we played the game a million times, added up the number of times you threw the dice and divided by one million, I'm quite sure that the result would be closer to 36 than to any other whole number. The mean has this long run statistical stability and upon this stability is based the financial security of casinos!

It's very simple to calculate the mean waiting time, or *average* number of trials, necessary for an event to occur. Merely invert the probability of the event, that is, take its reciprocal. Thus the average number of tosses of the dice to produce eleven will be 18 and the average number of spins of the roulette wheel necessary for us to observe 00 will be 38. Unlike the Gambler's Rule for finding the median which is inaccurate if the event you're awaiting is too probable, this rule always works. So the average number of tosses of a coin to produce a head will be two and the average number of rolls of a die to get a four will be six.

A simple proof of this proposition results from using only elementary algebra and probabilistic reasoning. If we let p stand for the probability of the event whose occurrence we are awaiting and E stand for the expected number of trials until it does occur, then

$$E = p \times 1 + (1 - p) \times (1 + E)$$

since with probability p it takes only one trial and with probability 1 – p we have used up one trial and are starting from scratch. Solving the equation gives E = 1/p.

Birthdays in the Next Issue

Fortified with this pleasant knowledge it should be child's play for you to determine how many people you must stop on the street to find someone whose birthday (but not year) matches yours. Also, imagine that a million people throughout the world performed the same experiment and reported their results to you. If you added up the results and divided by a million, what number would the resultant quotient be near?

Here's something else to think about until the next issue when I'll discuss birthday problems at greater length. How many people would you have to gather in a room (or in an auditorium) to have at least an even chance of having all 365 birthdays represented? (For simplicity we ignore anybody admitting to having been born on February 29.) I promise you the answer next time.

4

MEANS AND MEDIANS OF WAITING DISTRIBUTIONS

In the last issue of *C&S* the reader was left with the assignment of stopping people on the street until he found somebody whose birthday matched his own. (All birthdays are assumed to be different from February 29.)

Those of you who applied the Old Gambler's Rule by multiplying $365 \times .693$ correctly concluded that 253 was the *median* of the distribution, namely the smallest number of people which would give you a better than even chance of matching your birthday. The actual probability of getting at least one match of your birthday with 253 people interviewed is

$$1 - \left(\frac{364}{365}\right)^{253} = .5005,$$

while for 252 people we have

$$1 - \left(\frac{364}{365}\right)^{252} = .4991.$$

Incidentally, there's a modification of the Old Gambler's Rule which will usually produce a very accurate estimate of the median waiting time even when the event you're waiting for is not too improbable. The modification is this:

Express the probability of the awaited event with a numerator of one (this will usually already be the case anyway); subtract .5 from the denominator of the probability so expressed; then multiply this resultant quantity by .693.

Thus, to find the number of tosses of a die necessary to give at least a 50% chance of a four appearing, we take .5 from six, since six is the denominator of 1/6, the probability of a four appearing on any roll. $5.5 \times .693 = 3.81$ indicates correctly that three tosses will not be enough, but that four tosses will.

The median number of spins of a roulette wheel needed to produce double zero is similarly arrived at by multiplying $37.5 \times .693 = 25.99$, which not only identifies 26 as the necessary number of spins, but also shows that it is just barely sufficient to give a better than even chance:

$$1 - \left({}^{37}\!/_{38} \right)^{26} = .5001$$

A secondary question was: What would be the average number of people for the millions of *C&S* readers to have to interview before finding that first birthday match? While it's more likely than not to have achieved success after checking out 253 people, it's also possible to have to wait a very long time; in about 5% of the cases a match wouldn't have occurred until sometime after the first 1100 people were asked.

What we're asking for here is the *mean* of the distribution. If you added up the number of people interviewed until the first match occurred, for millions of individuals performing this experiment, and then divided by that number of individuals performing the experiment, the resultant quotient would be very close to 365. The average waiting time, it was pointed out in the last issue, could be calculated by merely inverting the probability of success on any trial. In the birthday example we take the reciprocal of 1/365 to get our mean.

How Many People to Get All Birthdays?

Now for something new. Recall the challenge at the end of last issue's article: How many people would you have to gather in a room to have at least an even chance that all 365 birthdays would be represented? What did you guess? I hope not 730 since, with 730 people, the odds are more than millions of millions to one against the event taking place.

You probably sense that what we're after here is a median, rather than a mean, waiting time. And yet our Old Gambler's Rule will be of no use to us because we're not dealing with a single improbable event, but rather with many events, most of which are quite probable.

Let me explain. After the first person enters the room we will then be waiting for another person to come in who has a separate birthday from the first one. If this were a problem of means we would now be on our way to a solution. The chance that a newly entering person

29

has a different birthday from the first birthday is 364/365; hence we *expect* to wait for 365/364 people in order to get that second birthday covered.

Now, imagine we've already covered two birthdays. How long (how many people) do we expect to have to wait until that third birthday arrives? On the average it will be the reciprocal of 363/365, or 365/363. Once we have covered all but one birthday we will probably have to wait a long time to get the last one. How long? On the *average* it will be 365 people.

We haven't come up with an answer to the original problem about the *median* number of people required to cover all the birthdays but we have solved a related one, namely, we can calculate the *mean* number required. Thinking of this experiment taking place in hundreds of thousands of rooms, auditoriums, or amphitheatres throughout the world, we have determined that the average number of people necessary to represent all 365 birthdays will be

$$1 + \frac{365}{364} + \frac{365}{363} + \frac{365}{362} + \ldots + \frac{365}{2} + \frac{365}{1} =$$

$$365\left(\frac{1}{365} + \frac{1}{364} + \frac{1}{363} + \frac{1}{362} + \ldots + \frac{1}{2} + \frac{1}{1}\right) = 2364.65.$$

Similarly, the average number of tosses of a coin for both sides to appear is $2 \times (1/2 + 1/1) = 3$. What would be the average number of spins of a roulette wheel required for the ball to have fallen into all 38 frets? How many times, on the average, would a die have to be rolled for all six faces to appear? Make a guess before performing the calculations; you may be surprised at the results.

But How Can We Find the Median?

We have digressed, of course, to solve a problem that was simpler than our original one. We wanted to know how many people would be necessary in order to have at least an even chance of covering all the birthdays. Since the mean number of 2364.65 is heavily influenced by some occasional cases when it might be necessary to have more than 5,000 people, we'd expect the median to be somewhat smaller than 2365, as it usually is in skewed distributions of this type. But how much smaller? Again, perhaps it will help to revert to a simpler problem.

What is the median number of tosses of a coin to produce both sides? The first toss always must be made, and then we'll have exactly an even chance of tossing the other side on the second toss. Therefore, two is the median: we have at least an even (in fact, *exactly* an even) chance of getting both sides in two tosses of the coin.

Unfortunately, the multifacetedness of something even as simple as a die quickly blunts this approach and we have to resort to some tricky symbolism to prevail. Consider the problem of finding the smallest number of tosses of a die to have at least an even chance that all six faces will have appeared.

Let $P(1, 1) = 1$ be the probability that one die produces one face. This is self-evident trivia. One die always produces one face; that's a *certainty*

31

(which is what we've said by assigning the probability of one).

Let P(2, 1) = 1/6 be the probability that two dice produce one face. This is 1/6 because it's the same as the chance that the second die matches the first. P(2, 2) = 5/6 is the probability that two tosses yield two faces and is 5/6 because that's the chance that the second toss differs from the first.

Now P(3,1) = $(1/6)^2$ = 1/36, the chance that the first three rolls produce only one number. But watch how I calculate P(3, 2), namely the probability that three tosses produce exactly two distinct faces:

$$P(3,2) = \frac{2}{6} \times P(2,2) + \frac{5}{6} \times P(2,1) = \frac{2}{6} \times \frac{5}{6} + \frac{5}{6} \times \frac{1}{6} = \frac{15}{36}$$

And P(3, 3) = 4/6 × P(2, 2) = 4/6 × 5/6 = 20/36 is the probability of three dice producing three distinct faces. This could have been found directly as 5/6 × 4/6, the chance that the second toss differs from the first times the chance that the third toss differs from the first two, but I wish to emphasize this method of recurrence, namely calculation by using previously calculated numbers.

One more example before I turn you loose on your own to solve the dice problem:

$$P(4,2) = \frac{2}{6} \times P(3,2) + \frac{5}{6} \times P(3,1) = \frac{2}{6} \times \frac{15}{36} + \frac{5}{6} \times \frac{1}{36} = \frac{35}{216}$$

If we let P(N, J) stand for the probability that N dice show J different faces, then we may use the relation

$$P(N,J) = \frac{J}{6} \times P(N-1,J) + \frac{(7-J)}{6} \times P(N-1,J-1)$$

to successively build up all of these numbers. What we're interested in is P(N, 6), the probability that all six faces appear when N dice are thrown. In particular, for what value of N does this probability first exceed 1/2?

This same method can be applied to the problem of finding the median number of trials for all possible results to have occurred in either the roulette or birthday example. There are so many calculations, however, that a computer's assistance must be enlisted. The results appear in the following displays:

ROULETTE	
Number of Spins	Chance Ball Has Fallen in All 38 Compartments
38	.0000000000000005
100	.0466
125	.2292
151	.4920
152	.5016
175	.6929
200	.8302
250	.9526
300	.9873
500	.9999

BIRTHDAY

Number of People in Room	Probability All Birthdays Occur
365	One chance out of 7 billion trillion quadrillion quintillion sextillion septillion octillion nonillion
1000	.0000000000017
1500	.0020
2000	.2161
2200	.4146
2286	.499414
2287	.500371
2500	.6805
3000	.9072
4000	.9938
5000	.9996

Next Time More Birthdays

Many readers have probably heard of the conventional, recently popularized, birthday problem: How many people do we need in a room to have at least an even chance that there are at least two matching birthdays among the people? The answer is surprisingly low: with 23 people in the room there is better than a 50% chance of some birthday match. (Of course, it's unlikely to be yours, or that of any other *prespecified* individual, which provides the match.)

Next time I'll show you how this is calculated. If we think of the people entering the room sequentially we can consider this, too, as a waiting time problem. Curiously the median number of people to get the first matching birthday (23 in this formulation) is now more easily calculated than the mean.

Between now and then, and with the previous result already known to you, speculate on these two questions: How many people do we need in a room in order to have a better than even chance of 1) having at least one triplication of birthdays (that is, a birthday shared by three or more people); and, 2) having at least two different birthdays each shared by two or more people?

5

MATCHING BIRTHDAZE

How can we show that 23 people are sufficient to have better than an even chance of providing at least one birthday match?

The multiplicity of ways that we can have at least one pair of matching birthdays makes a direct calculation of such a probability impractical. For instance, we could have exactly one pair, two pairs and a triplication, four pairs and two quadruplications, etc. Hence we consider a simpler, but related event.

The chance of *no* matching birthdays among n=23 people is calculated easily:

$$\underbrace{\frac{365}{365} \times \frac{364}{365} \times \frac{363}{365} \times \ldots \times \frac{343}{365}}_{23 \text{ factors}} = .49270$$

The second factor, 364/365, is the chance that the second person in the room has a different birthday from the first. 363/365 is then the chance that the third person has a different birthday from the first two, unalike, birthdays. We multiply another factor for each person in the room, reducing the numerator by one at each stage, since the number of permissible possibilities diminishes in the same fashion.

So now we know that the chance of at least one match is 1 − .49270 = .50730, although we haven't broken this latter figure down into its many component possibilities of occurrence. To show that 23 is the smallest number of people which gives us at least an even chance, we perform the same sort of computation for n=22 people:

$$\frac{365}{365} \times \frac{364}{365} \times \frac{363}{365} \times \ldots \times \frac{344}{365} = .52430,$$

so we see there is a better than even chance of *not* succeeding in this case.

Incidentally, the *mean* number of people necessary in a room to get a match (we can think of the people entering the room one by one and announcing their birthdays until a match takes place) is 24.6166, slightly larger than the median as is customary in this sort of problem. The calculations are tedious and unimportant, but the implication is that you might be able to set up a favorable bet with someone who knew that 23 was the median; offer him $24 if he agrees to pay you as many dollars as it requires people in the room to produce that first match.

At Least Two Matching Days

Now to the other two birthday problems posed in the last issue of *C&S*. First, how many people are necessary to have an even chance *that at least two days provide matching birthdays?*

This is a difficult problem to solve, far more difficult than the conventional birthday problem just discussed. What did you guess? The correct answer is 36, probably surprising to most people in its smallness.

Here, briefly, is how to arrive at the answer. First calculate the chance of *no matching birthday* for n people by the method previously displayed. Then find the probability of exactly *one pair of matching birthdays but no other match*; do this by multiplying the "no-match" probability by n(n−1) and dividing the result by two and by (366−n).

Next, find the chance of *exactly one triplication but no other match* by multiplying the previous chance of exactly one pair by (n − 2) and then dividing by three and by (367 − n). Following this, find the probability of *one quadruplication and no other match* by multiplying the triplication probability by (n − 3) and then dividing by four and by (368 − n). Here's how it goes for n=36:

$$P[\text{no match}] = \frac{365}{365} \times \frac{364}{365} \times \frac{363}{365} \times \ldots \times \frac{330}{365} \qquad = .16782$$

$$P[\text{one pair, nothing else}] = \frac{n(n-1) \times .16782}{2(366-n)} = \frac{36 \times 35 \times .16782}{2(330)} \qquad = .32038$$

$$P[\text{only triplication}] = \frac{(n-2) \times .320380}{3(367-n)} = \frac{34 \times .320380}{3(331)} \qquad = .01097$$

$$P[\text{only quadruplication}] = \frac{(n-3) \times .01097}{4(368-n)} = \frac{33 \times .01097}{4(332)} \qquad = .00027$$

$$P[\text{only quintuplication}] = \frac{(n-4) \times .00027}{5(369-n)} = \frac{32 \times .00027}{5(333)} \qquad = .00001$$

Total   .49945

We stop here and total because our next calculation, of exactly one sextuplication of birth-

39

days and no other matches, will be .00000, rounded to the accuracy we are using. Now, .49945 is the chance that either *no* days provide a match or only a *single* day provides a (possibly multiple) match.

Therefore, 1 – .49945 = .50055 is the chance of having matches on at least two days with 36 people. For n=35 people a similar computation would give 1 – .53060 = .46940, so 36 is the smallest number of people which will give at least an even chance of success.

Three or More People on the Same Day

To solve the problem of how many people are required to give at least a 50% chance of having a triple match, a similar but even more laborious set of calculations is performed. As before we begin with the probabilities of no match and of exactly one matching pair but no other match.

We then take a different direction by calculating P_{j+1}, the probability of exactly $j + 1$ matched *pairs* but no other matches, by using the relation:

$$P_{j+1} = \frac{(n - 2j)(n - 2j - 1) \times P_j}{2(j + 1)(365 + j - n)}$$

All of these numbers are added to produce the chance that n people have no match or just paired matches. This probability is subtracted from one to yield the probability of a triplication (or higher order matching) taking place. This sort of mindless and time consuming arithmetic is best reserved for computers.

For 87 people the chance of triplication is .49946, while with 88 people the probability of getting three or more people with the same birthday becomes .51106, greater than 50% for the first time. What did you guess?

I sense that this session has been a mite too technical, too computational, so next time we'll take up something a little more in a gambling context. We all know that the chance of tossing double sixes with a pair of dice is 1/36. Also, the chance of a total of seven is 1/6, so the chance of tossing consecutive totals of seven in two rolls is also 1/36.

Suppose a pair of dice is tossed repeatedly. Whenever a pair of sixes occurs Mr. A wins a dollar and whenever two *consecutive* totals of seven appear Mr. B wins a dollar. Who, if anybody, has the edge in this dice proposition.

6

A PARADOXICAL PROPOSITION

Boxcars or two consecutive totals of seven? An enterprising pair from New York was offering this proposition in Atlantic City. Unfortunately they had the wrong side of the bet!

You have your choice of betting that a pair of sixes will appear on a roll of the dice before back-to-back totals of seven occur; or, taking the other side, that two *consecutive* totals of seven appear before a single roll of double sixes. The chance of a single roll producing (66) is 1/36 and the chance of two straight totals of seven is also $1/36 = 1/6 \times 1/6$. Which side would you take?

Also, would it make any difference if the dice were tossed repeatedly until one side had won the best two out of three or best three out of five? What about the long run, imagining the contest to go on forever between two inexhaustible gamblers?

For convenience of reference we'll assume Mr. A bets on double sixes and Mr. B bets that the back-to-back totals of seven occur. We'll calculate A's chance of winning the first encounter. A trick will enable us to avoid the mathematics of the infinite.

43

The symbolism of mathematics is both useful and indispensable here. We assign the letter p to stand for the probability that A wins. We can find p by solving the following equation:

$$p = \frac{1}{36} + \frac{29}{36} \times p + \frac{6}{36} \times \frac{1}{36} + \frac{6}{36} \times \frac{29}{36} \times p$$

The equation can be translated into words to justify its appropriateness. "The chance A wins is the chance that either he tosses (66) on the first toss, or he throws a neutral total (neither twelve nor seven) on the first toss and subsequently wins, or he tosses seven on the first toss and twelve on the next roll, or he tosses seven on the first toss, a neutral total on the second toss, and then he subsequently wins."

Notice how each "+" in the equation is translated into the conjunction "or" and each "×" becomes an "and." Years of teaching experience have convinced me that careful use of language is indispensable for solving probability problems.

Getting back to our equation, we can solve it by multiplying both sides by 216, obtaining:

$$216\,p = 6 + 174\,p + 1 + 29\,p$$

$$13\,p = 7$$

$$p = \frac{7}{13} = .538$$

Thus Mr. A is a seven to six favorite to win the first encounter. Yet the people offering the proposition wanted to bet on the consecutive sevens, that is, to take our Mr. B's side! What did they have in mind?

A Buildup of Consecutive Sevens

Possibly their intuition held that both sides had the same chance of winning the first decision, but that *if* Mr. B won at any time he would have the potential to develop several wins in a row by a streak of totals of seven. For example, four consecutive totals of seven would produce three wins for them if the game continued beyond the first decided encounter. But would this accumulation of wins give them an edge?

We've already seen the fallacy of the belief that both sides are equally likely to win the first decision since p=7/13 was found to be A's chance initially. To investigate what happens as the game progresses we must discover A's chance of winning the next time if the previous toss was a seven and it carries over as a possibility for B to win on the very next toss with another seven.

In this case A's *conditional* chance of winning the *next* encounter is:

$$\frac{1}{36} + \frac{29}{36} \times p =$$

$$\frac{1}{36} + \frac{29}{36} \times \frac{7}{13} =$$

$$\frac{13}{468} + \frac{203}{468} =$$

$$\frac{216}{468} = \frac{6}{13}$$

The justification for this is that A must win on the next toss or else the next roll must be neutral in which case A's position reverts to what it was initially.

To calculate the chance of any particular sequence of results, remember that, if A won the previous time he has a 7/13 chance to win the next time, whereas if A lost the last one his chance of winning the next is only 6/13. Thus the probability of A winning the best two out of three can be tabulated as:

Sequence	Probability				
AA	7/13	×	7/13		= 637/2197
ABA	7/13	×	6/13	× 6/13	= 252/2197
BAA	6/13	×	6/13	× 7/13	= 252/2197
Total	1141/2197				= .519

More lengthy calculations show that A's chance of winning the best three out of five decreases to .514. In fact A's initial advantage begins to die out as we shall see next.

The Long Run

A's chances of winning the first several decided contests are:

First					=	7/13	=.5384615
Second	7/13	× 7/13 +	6/13	× 6/13 =	85/169		=.5029586
Third	85/169	× 7/13 +	84/169	× 6/13 =	1099/2197		=.5002276
Fourth	1099/2197	× 7/13 +	1098/2197	× 6/13 =	14281/28561		=.5000175

Although A's probability of winning continues to decrease, it remains greater than B's for each decision. It can be shown that A's chance of winning the mth contest is $(1 + 1/13^m)/2$. Thus A begins with an advantage and maintains an, albeit diminishing, edge throughout eternity.

Suppose the dice will be rolled many, many times. We can gain some insight into B's improved long run prospect by calculating the chances that each contestant wins on, for instance, the 1800th roll of the dice.

A's chance of winning then is, of course, 1/36, the chance of double sixes being tossed. B's probability of winning specifically on the 1800th roll is the chance that the 1799th toss *was* a seven and the 1800th *will be* a seven also. This is $6/36 \times 6/36 = 1/36$, the same as A's chance of winning on this prespecified trial. In fact the same equal chance prevails for both of them winning on any trial *after* the first!

What's mildly paradoxical in this equality of chances on the 1800th roll is that we expect there to be something like 100 resolved contests by this time and our attention returns to $(1 + 1/13^{100})/2$, or thereabouts, as A's probability of winning, establishing him as a slight favorite.

Who Will Win Next?

Perhaps even more stunning, after we've accepted the relative equality of A and B once the lengthy sequence of tosses is under way, is that A remains a distinct favorite to win the *next* contest if we look in on the gamble at any random time in the future! To see this imagine we begin observing after the millionth roll and then wait for

47

the next winner. A's chance of winning *next* is

$$5/6 \times 7/13 + 1/6 \times 6/13 = 41/78,$$

since either the previous (millionth) toss was a non-seven and we're back to scratch, or it was a seven and A has a 6/13 chance of going on to win.

Other Strangeness

If they agree to play for exactly 18,000 rolls of the dice, but no longer, A has a total expected earning of $1/36 = 2.78\%$ of a betting unit. His total expected earning remains the same whether they agree to extend the contest to 18 billion tosses, or even reduce it to one throw of the dice.

If they agree to play until exactly 1000 contests have been resolved (which should take about 18,000 rolls), A has a total expected earning of $(1 - 1/13^{1000})/12 = 8.33\%$ of a betting unit.

The game can be made fair for B (zero expectation for both) if A agrees to quit as soon as he has won one contest! In fact this is a game in which the participants should quit after a loss rather than after a win.

7

SHOULD YOU GAMBLE IF THEY GIVE BACK HALF YOUR LOSSES?

The topic for this issue was suggested in a phone call from a former Indonesian casino owner. Unfortunately, before he could contract and compensate me for my services, his casino was closed. Apparently this was due to his failure to offer the required *mordida* to the appropriate local officials.

The problems and adventures of this colorful international gambling figure notwithstanding, let's get to the question he asked. He wanted to induce local gamblers to play at his casino by offering them half their money back if they lost and he wondered how long he'd have to require them to play in order to have a mathematical advantage, and what sort of an advantage it would be.

Let's imagine the bet is an even money one on color (either red or black) at roulette. It's obvious that the casino could not afford to refund half the gambler's losses after every coup (spin, in roulette) since then the expectation would be in favor of the player,

$$1 \times \frac{18}{38} - \frac{1}{2} \times \frac{20}{38} = \frac{8}{38} = 21.05\%$$

instead of the usual

$$1 \times \frac{18}{38} - 1 \times \frac{20}{38} = \frac{-2}{38} = -5.26\%.$$

At the other extreme the house might require the gambler to play for such a long time (before invoking the settlement on the basis of either all his winnings or half his losses) that the "law of large numbers" would virtually guarantee that the house won, and won at the expected rate of 5.26%. In this case, *after the settlement*, the player would have lost to be sure, but at 2.63%, which is half the usual rate.

Practicalities being what they are, the duration of play would probably be defined as an evening, or perhaps a week. So we're back to our original question: what is the minimum number of coups necessary to guarantee that the house has at least an even break? From the previous discussion we know that the answer must be greater than one but less than infinity.

Before continuing the article, which presents an exposition of the solution, the reader should try to guess what the result would be. Also, would it make any difference if the game was craps rather than roulette? Or would a different bet in roulette alter this minimum number of plays necessary to destroy the player's initial edge on a single bet?

Surprisingly, the device which facilitates answering these questions can be found in the works of the exceptionally personable, talented, and modest author of that gambling classic *The Theory of Blackjack*. It is the greatly overlooked and underrated "Unit Normal Linear Loss Integral" [UNLLI] which appears on page 87 of the previously cited tome.

A piece of mathematics (which is at the same time too sophisticated for this rag and too trivial for statistical journals) informs us that the standard deviation score which has corresponding entry for its UNLLI equal to itself is the key to our problem! A glance at the tables reveals to us that the magic number is, approximately, .276. The minimal number of coups, n, which guarantees the casino to be even, with this half-refund of potential losses, is that number for which the player's break even position after n plays is .276 standard deviations above his expected loss.

Here's how to solve for the answer to the roulette problem, now. After n plays the player "expects" to be $n \times 2/38 = n/19$ units behind. The standard deviation for n plays is the square root of the "variance" for n plays, which in turn is n times the variance for a single play of the game. For all practical purposes the variance of an individual result may be taken to be the average squared result. Betting on red once results in either +1 (a win) or –1 (a loss) and in either case the squared result is +1, and hence the variance may be taken as +1.

Summarizing:

Variance of one play = 1

Variance of n plays = $n \times 1 = n$

Standard deviation of n plays = $\sqrt{\text{Variance of n plays}} = \sqrt{n}$

Standardizing the break even point is done by dividing the n/19 units which the player must be above average by the standard deviation of $\sqrt{n}$. This "standard score" is usually designated by the letter "z".

$$z = \frac{n/19}{\sqrt{n}} = \frac{\sqrt{n}}{19}$$

Now, to find the guaranteeing value of n we merely equate

$$\frac{\sqrt{n}}{19} = .276$$

and solve for

$$n = (.276 \times 19)^2 = 27.5.$$

In fact, exact calculations by a computer show that for a 27 coup session, with the player receiving half his losses back, his expected gain is 1.8% of a unit and with 28 spins the player expects to lose 1.9% of a unit, so the UNLLI has done its job quite well indeed here.

For craps the player's expected loss after n plays is $n \times 28/1980 = 7n/495$. Since the player wins or loses one unit at a time as in the color bet for roulette, his standard deviation for n plays will again be $\sqrt{n}$. Standardizing,

$$z = \frac{7n/495}{\sqrt{n}} = \frac{7\sqrt{n}}{495}, \text{ and equating}$$

$$\frac{7\sqrt{n}}{495} = .276, \text{ we find}$$

$$n = 380.7.$$

Here the UNLLI betrays us a little since it actually takes 382 trials to shift the edge to the casino which refunds half the player's loss, the gambler having a marginal advantage if a session consists of 381 games of craps.

Now, would you believe that a wealthy Arab oil sheik recently approached an unnamed Las Vegas casino with a proposition along these lines: he said that he just loved to play roulette but he lamented the fact that he always lost and asked if the casino would refund half his losses at the end of the evening. The casino said yes, that if he'd bet $10,000 a shot on roulette he could have anything he wanted. They did insist, however, that he bet on at least 38 spins (an intuitive figure apparently) for the evening.

The sheik then consulted an anonymous pundit (a highly-personable, talented, and modest veteran of the Vegas scene, I might add) and returned to the casino with the suggestion that play be even lengthier, 234 coups if possible, so long as he could bet his $10,000 any way he desired. The casino, needless to say, was delighted to accept and rolled out the magic carpet. The rest is, of course, legend. The sheik played on merrily for 100 Arabian nights, averaging $87,967.60 profit for each session. What had happened?

What happened was that the sheik bet on a number (actually 00) rather than color! The effect was to greatly increase his variance, although his conventional expectation per play remained

$$\frac{35 \times 1 \ -1 \times 37}{38} = \frac{-2}{38}, \text{ a loss.}$$

The average squared result on one play now becomes

$$35^2 \times \frac{1}{38} + (-1)^2 \times \frac{37}{38} = \frac{1262}{38} = 33.2 \text{ rather than } 1.$$

Hence, the standard deviation for n plays is about $\sqrt{33.2n}$, and by our previous technique the number of coups necessary for the casino to break even when guaranteeing the sheik half his losses after n plays is approximately the solution to

$$\frac{n/19}{\sqrt{33.2n}} = .276, \text{ which is } n = 912.$$

Precise (but, I would remind you, very expensive) calculations show that 930 plays would in fact be necessary for the casino to gain the edge.

Not only did the sheik have an advantage, but he truly had "the best of it" in that his shrewd selection of 234 spins per session was designed to maximize his total potential profit for the evening. Even more obscure mathematics than that alluded to earlier establishes that the player's greatest possible gain occurs for approximately one fourth the number of coups necessary to make the "half back if you lose" proposition an even gamble for each side.

That maximal total profit itself can be shown to be about 72% of the expected loss for the same number of trials if there were no bonus rebate. As an example, 8.7976 units is approximately 72% of the expected loss for 234 trials, namely $234/19 = 12.32$ units.

Here's a table summarizing our findings for this arrangement where the house refunds half the player's losses at the end of the session:

	Craps	Color in Roulette	Number in Roulette
Number of coups for house to gain edge	382	28	930
Number of coups for player to have greatest expectation	93	7	234
Player's expected profit (in units) for number of trials (above) guaranteeing him maximal profit.	.96016	.27510	8.79676

You might test your understanding by working out the same figures for the various proposition bets on the crap table or the inside-outside bet in roulette.

In the summer of 1990, I was told that several Las Vegas casinos have an informal policy of refunding 10% of the gambling loss per trip for certain high-rolling clientele. Because such an agreement is informal and hence not binding, there is really no way to guarantee exploitation of the situation. It is interesting, however, to work out the possibilities for a small number of trials.

Suppose the gambler plays n coups, winning or losing one unit with probabilities respectively of p and $q = 1 - p$. Then his conventional expectation is $n(p - q)$, while the amount he expects to accrue from the refund is:

$$B = \sum_{k=0}^{n/2} \binom{n}{k} p^k q^{n-k} (n-2k)/10.$$

The gambler's total trip expectation is $n(p - q) + B$, where B is the 10% refund bonus above.

If $p = .4929$ (craps), the gambler has a positive trip expectation for $n = 11$ or fewer coups, with maximal expectation of .036 units for $n = 3$ plays. Supposing $p = .4942$ (baccarat), there will be a positive expectation for $n = 17$ or fewer coups, $n = 3$ again providing the maximum expectation, in this case .043 units. Also, an odd number of coups is preferable to an even number one less than it.

If we investigate the more volatile number bet in roulette, which does not have unit payoff but rather is 35 to 1, we see that greater profits and longer playing time with positive expectation are possible, despite the inherently poorer expectation than in craps or baccarat. The trip expectation for n bets on a single number, with 10% refund of any loss is

$$\sum_{k=0}^{n/36} \binom{n}{k} \left(\frac{1}{38}\right)^k \left(\frac{37}{38}\right)^{n-k} (n - 36k)/10 - n/19.$$

This maximizes at +.241 units for $n = 11$ coups, and is still positive for $n = 24$ wagers, before turning negative forever after.

In the next issue I'll show how the mathematical idea of a "random walk" can be used to determine how often a successful gambler's capital is at an all-time high. We will use a little geometric trick to identify this probability with the gambler's chance of never falling behind.

8

AN ALL-TIME HIGH — HOW OFTEN?

In his meticulous *Professional Blackjack*, Stanford Wong cautions the gambler not to be discouraged by comparing his current fortune with what it had been previously. Wong correctly opines that even a successful gambler will rarely be currently at a new all-time high in his earnings. In this issue we'll derive the long run chance of a gambler's fortune being instantaneously higher than it ever was before.

Random Walk

An ingenious mathematical contrivance which enables us to study phenomena of this type is a *random walk.* Imagine you're waiting for somebody on a sidewalk constructed with regularly separated blocks of concrete, about four and a half feet long in most residential areas. To pass the time you decide to toss a coin, proceeding east one square if the result is a head and west one square if you get a tail.

What are some of the mathematical characteristics of this random walk (for such an odyssey it truly is)? In particular, is it possible that you will never return to your starting point to meet your friend? And if you do return, how long do you expect it to take you to get back?

Mathematics produces answers to these questions by imagining an infinitely long block, called a *number scale,* with locations, called *integers,* analogous to the squares of our sidewalk. The scale extends forever in both directions; the middle point, called the *origin,* is designated as the number zero, while positive numbers are those to the right (east) and negative numbers designate the locations to the left (west) of zero.

```
...●    ●    ●    ●    ●    ●    ●  ...
   -3   -2   -1    0   +1   +2   +3
```

It has been shown for such an ideal random walk, conducted with a *fair* coin having equal probabilities of 1/2 for both heads and tails, that the walker is indeed certain to return to the origin, or zero point, where he started. However, the average time before return is infinite! This is quite a startling result in light of the easily calculated fact that we have a 50% chance of returning to where we started after only two steps: the second toss need only be opposite to what the first was. The following chart displays selected probabilities of returning to the origin for the first time after various numbers of steps.

X = number of steps	P(X) = Chance of first return at step X	Cumulative sum of P(X)	Cumulative sum of X • P(X)
2	.500000	.5000	1.0000
4	.125000	.6250	1.5000
6	.062500	.6875	1.8750
8	.039062	.7266	2.1875
10	.027338	.7539	2.4609
64	.001577	.9007	6.3582
256	.000195	.9502	12.7537
1000	.000025	.9748	25.2250
6000	.000002	.9897	61.8013

In the column entitled "Cumulative sum of P(X)" we find the probability of having returned to our starting point on or before X steps. The certainty of return is reflected by this column's evident convergence to 1.0000. The infinite "expected time" for return to the origin would be reflected by the unbounded growth of "Cumulative sum of X·P(X)." As can be seen from the chart the limitless magnitude of this quantity is not so evident yet; the greatest contributions to this infinite expected time come from the extremely improbable first returns in more than 6000 steps.

The notion of a random walk can be extended to two dimensions by imagining a tiled grid such as can be seen on the floors of some public restrooms. Suppose a card is selected from an ordinary deck, with a spade requiring one step north, a heart one step east, a diamond one step to the south, and a club one step to the west. (Be careful to replace the card before the next one is chosen; otherwise you're *guaranteed* to be back where you started at least every 52 steps.) Although it seems less likely than in our one dimensional random walk, a return to the origin is again certain to occur. The expected time is, of course, infinite.

A set of monkey bars on a children's playground illustrates the possibility of introducing a third dimension, namely up or down, to random walks. A standard die could provide equal probabilities of moving either up, down, north, south, east, or west. It is not until we put our walk into this third dimension that failure to return to the origin becomes possible. Very advanced mathematics has established that the chance of ever returning to the starting point in such a three dimensional random walk is .340537. Hence about 2/3 of the time our random walker (or climber, in this instance) wanders forever without returning home.

Although it's difficult to imagine realistic physical circumstances for random walks in higher dimensions, such things do exist in the realm of mathematics. We might think of time as being a fourth dimension, but its measurement would have to be discrete (moving into the future or past by exact increments, such as one minute precisely). Four, five, and six dimensional random walks have associated probabilities of returning to the origin of .193202, .135179, and .104715, while for higher dimension d, the formula $1/2(d - 1)$ is a good approximation. In analogy to the cubic die, regular solids like the dodecahedron (12 sides for six dimensions) and the icosahedron (20 sides for ten dimensions) could be used in some cases to determine the motion.

One Dimensional Random Walk as a Model for Gambling Problems

We can think of the locations on the number scale as representing how much a gambler, involved in a game at each play of which he either wins or loses one unit, is currently behind (negative) or ahead (positive). Zero, of course, represents being even.

What we have just learned is that, if the chance of winning is equal to the chance of losing ("symmetric random walk" is the term used when motion in either direction is equiprobable), then the gambler is certain to return to the fortune he started with. It may, however, take a very long time for this to occur. It can also be shown that such a gambler is certain to achieve every possible state of fortune ultimately; at some time he'll be 273 units below zero and at some other time he will have won 777,777 units.

But what happens if the game is not equitable, if the chance of winning is unequal to the chance of losing? The "law of large numbers" assures us that the player with better than even chance of winning an individual encounter must ultimately prevail. What, though, is the chance of never being behind, or, almost the same thing, always being ahead?

Let the favorite have a probability designated by p of winning each game, where p is greater than 1/2. (The casino which banks roulette bets on color has a value of p = 20/38; p = 251/495 characterizes the house situation for craps.) Suppose x stands for the chance of always being ahead after the first toss and y denotes the probability of never being behind, the distinction being that y includes the possibility of returning to even, but not falling behind.

We can write two equations whose simultaneous solution will yield the unknown values of x and y:

1) $x = py$
2) $y = x + p(1 - y)y$.

The first equation states that to always be ahead, one must win the first game and then never fall behind from that new position of being one unit ahead. The second equation expresses the notion that either you're always ahead (x) or you win the first game (p), then do not never fall behind from your position one unit ahead (1 – y), and subsequently never fall behind your original starting point. The seeming grammatical lapse is intentional: to "not never fall behind from...one unit ahead" is to necessarily back up to zero for a first time.

The equations are easily solved, yielding

$$y = 2 - 1/p \quad \text{and} \quad x = 2p - 1.$$

These figures have interesting interpretations for the examples where the casino was banking roulette or craps. Letting $p = 20/38$, we have $y = 2 - 38/20 = 1/10$ and $x = 2 \times 20/38 - 1 = 1/19$. Since the casino has a $1/10$ chance of never being behind, the player must have a $1 - 1/10 = 9/10$ chance of getting ahead at least once. Hence the roulette player who bets a dollar at a time on red *until he is one dollar ahead* has a 90% chance of achieving that goal, assuming he has limitless capital to begin with. Similarly, for craps bets the casino success probability of $p = 251/495$ translates into $y = 2 - 495/251 = 7/251$. This gives the infinitely wealthy craps bettor a chance of $244/251 = 97\%$ of getting at least one bet ahead at some time in the play.

Chance of Being at an All Time High

We shall use a little geometric trick to show how the previous results can give an answer to the question posed at the beginning of the article: *what is the long run chance of a gambler's fortune being at an all time high?* First we must assume that the gambler's chance of winning an individual encounter is some value of p at least equal to 1/2, for otherwise the law of large numbers guarantees that the gambler's fortune will in fact diminish.

On the next page we sketch three possible paths for the gambler's fortune as time unfolds. Imagine that the three possible final positions, H, S, and X, are all positive and equal as the graphs show. Further suppose that these three positions are achieved after the same long period of time.

Note what characterizes the three paths. In case H the gambler always was ahead, in case S the gambler wasn't always ahead but never did fall behind, while in the bottom case X the gambler was behind for a certain period of time.

Now we play our trick. Turn this book upside down 180° and look at these three paths again! Regard X, S, and H as the starting points and the three former zero points as the locations (positive since zero is now above the starting point) of the gambler's fortune after a long period of time. The now top graph X depicts a gambler who is not currently at an all time high. The middle graph S illustrates a gambler who is at an all time high, albeit one he achieved, but never surpassed, before. The bottom graph H shows the path of a satisfied gambler who retired at a brand new all time high.

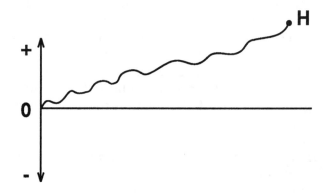

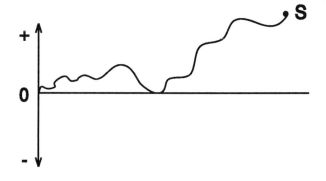

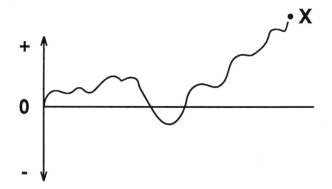

When we recognize that the upside down, backward, paths are equally as probable as the right side up, restored, paths we recognize the solutions to our problem. First, the chance of being at a new all time high sometime long into the future is the same as the chance of always being ahead, $x = 2p - 1$, which incidentally is also the gambler's expectation per play. Secondly, the chance of being at an all time high, but *possibly* having achieved it before, is $y = 2 - 1/p$.

These figures can, of course, also be interpreted as all time lows for gamblers playing unfavorable games. Just as $1/10$ is the chance that a casino banking roulette will be at an all time high, so too must it be the chance that the roulette player is at an all time low. Perhaps that's the attraction of betting on roulette; certainly you lose, but the odds are nine to one you can point to a time in the past when you were worse off than you are now!

There's another, intuitive, explanation for the gambler's expectation also being his chance of being currently at an all time high. After a large number, N, of plays he expects to have won $N(2p - 1)$ units. His current position is probably quite close to this ideal figure and he probably hasn't ever been too far above it. Hence, he has reached approximately $N(2p - 1)$ *new* levels of wealth in his gamble of N plays. The relative frequency of being at a new plateau, then, is $N(2p - 1)/N = 2p - 1$.

Next Time Games with Variable Payoffs

All of this previous discussion has been based on the assumption that exactly one unit changes hands, win or lose. Many gambling games, most notably blackjack and some of the other roulette bets, are not like this. Next time, I'll show how to modify these methods, as well as some of the conventional gambler's ruin formulas so well explicated in Wilson's *Casino Gambler's Guide*, when the payoffs are variable.

9

GAMBLER'S RUIN FORMULAS FOR NON-UNIT PAYOFFS

In the last issue of *C&S* two formulas were derived to describe different aspects of a gambler's fortune. Both formulas were based on the assumption that the gambler either won or lost exactly one unit at each play of the game. Letting p stand for the probability that the gambler wins one unit on a single play, we showed that:

x = 2p – 1 is the chance the gambler is always ahead and also is the long run probability that the gambler will be currently at a new all time high in his fortune, while

y = 2 – 1/p is the chance that the gambler never falls behind.

These formulas only make sense if p is at least 1/2, that is if the gambler has at least an even chance to win each play for one unit. Otherwise, if the gambler is at a disadvantage, both x and y will be equal to zero.

We can modify the second formula, y = 2 – 1/p, to produce an expression for the probability that a gambler starting with a units will never be ruined. As the formula stands, y gives the chance of never falling behind by a single unit. Hence

$1 - y = 1/p - 1$ must be the probability that the gambler does indeed drop back one unit at some time during his gamble.

Well, for our gambler with **a** initial units to be ultimately ruined he will have to first fall back one unit from his starting point of **a** units, then fall back another unit from that new level of fortune of a − 1 units, drop back another unit at some time from his fortune of a − 2 units, etc. The total probability of his falling back **a** units (one at a time, but not necessarily in **a** consecutive plays) must therefore be

$$\left(\frac{1}{p} - 1\right)^a = \left(\frac{1-p}{p}\right)^a = \left(\frac{q}{p}\right)^a$$

where the last expression, with q = 1 − p being the chance of losing an individual play, is the form most commonly encountered in the literature. Thus, with p = .6 and a = 3 as the gambler's initial fortune, his chance of ultimate ruin, if he is determined to play on forever in hopes of winning a limitless fortune, is

$$\left(\frac{.4}{.6}\right)^3 = \frac{8}{27} = .2963.$$

Chance of Ruin Before Doubling Fortune

Another similar formula that is easily derivable is the chance that a gambler will be ruined if his goal is more limited, he agreeing to stop the gamble as soon as he has doubled his previous fortune. Suppose, as before, our gambler is playing a game with single trial probability of winning equal to p = .6 and his goal is to turn his current fortune of a = 3 units into six units, at which time he resolves to quit. Let's look at some of the ways he can do this in terms of sequences of wins (W) and losses (L).

Sequences resulting in Doubling	Probability	
WWW	$(.6)^3$	= .2160
WWLWW	$(.6)^4 (.4)$	= .0518
LLWWWWW	$(.6)^5 (.4)^2$	= .0124
WLWWW	$(.6)^4 (.4)$	= .0518
. . . . .		

It now becomes apparent that there will be an infinity of such sequences having three more wins than losses, finishing with two wins, but allowing no possibility of having doubled the fortune previously in the sequence. Surely there must be an easier way of determining the gambler's total probability of doubling his capital before ruin. And there is!

Suppose we imagine another list displaying some of the sequences which result in the gambler being ruined. In particular, let us follow the pattern of our previous list, only interchanging W's with L's and L's with W's.

Sequences resulting in Ruin	Probability	
LLL	$(.4)^3$	= .0640
LLWLL	$(.4)^4 (.6)$	= .0154
WWLLLLL	$(.4)^5 (.6)^2$	= .0037
LWLLL	$(.4)^4 (.6)$	= .0154
. . . . .		

71

Notice that for every path leading to successful doubling of capital there is a corresponding path to ruin and that the relative magnitudes of the probabilities of these paths are to each other as $(.6)^3$ is to $(.4)^3$, or as .216 is to .064. It therefore follows that the total probability of doubling capital to probability of ruin must also be as .216 is to .064. Since the gambler is certain to do one or the other of these two things eventually, his chance of ruin must be

$$\frac{(.4)^3}{(.4)^3 + (.6)^3} = \frac{.064}{.280} = .2286$$

while his chance of doubling his capital is

$$\frac{(.6)^3}{(.4)^3 + (.6)^3} = \frac{.216}{.280} = .7714.$$

Note that his probability of ruin when he agrees to stop after doubling, .2286, is smaller than his previous chance of ruin, .2936, calculated when he attempts to play forever.

This reasoning leads us to another of the conventional gambler's ruin formulas, this one designed to give the chance of ruin for a gambler trying to double his capital beginning with a units and playing a game where he wins one unit with probability equal to p. By analogy, the probability of ruin is:

$$\frac{q^a}{q^a + p^a}$$

The two formulas,

$$\left(\frac{q}{p}\right)^a$$

for the chance of ultimate ruin playing forever and

$$\frac{q^a}{q^a + p^a}$$

for the chance of ruin before doubling capital, are two of the standards in most of the books, like Wilson's *Casino Gambler's Guide*, which treat this subject. What is presupposed, however, is that the game always results in the winning or losing of precisely one unit. Many real life gambles, such as number bets at roulette and blackjack with its occasional payoffs of 1.5, two, three, or four units, are not like this. How can we proceed in such a case?

Approximating Gambler's Ruin Formulas in Other Cases

Consider a roulette player trying to double a stake of 17 units. A bet on color gives a success probability of $p = 18/38$ with $q = 20/38$. Employment of the formula

$$\frac{p^a}{q^a + p^a}$$

shows the player's chance of doubling the stake before being ruined to be only .1429. Wouldn't it possibly be better to try betting on a number, say 00, even though the expectation per play is the same? Then one would have to lose 17 times in a row to be ruined and the chance of this is:

$$\left(\frac{37}{38}\right)^{17} = .6355;$$

hence the chance of doubling must be 1 − .6355 = .3645 which is considerably larger than the .1429 which applies to a color bet.

The preceding example shows that, when considering questions of gambler's ruin, two bets which happen to have the same expectation per play are not necessarily equivalent. What is required here is a method to use the standard gambler's ruin formulas in cases where the player may win or lose some amount other than a single unit. Since the actual solutions to such problems involve a rather advanced form of mathematics called "difference equations," I will propose a simple method of approximation which then enables use of the existing formulas.

The principle of the approximation is to replace the actual gamble by one which has the same expectation and average squared result, but in which only one unit changes hands at each step. This is done by assuming that the player bets a number of units equal to the square root of his average squared result and that his single trial probability of success is 1/2 plus half his expectation divided by the square root of his average squared result. We need some symbols here to write economically, so let EX stand for the player's expectation and EX^2 represent his average squared result. Our formula for the player's assumed single trial probability of success is:

$$p = \frac{1}{2} + \frac{EX}{2\sqrt{EX^2}}$$

For a bet on a number in roulette we have

$$EX = \frac{18}{38}(+1) + \frac{20}{38}(-1) = -\frac{1}{19} = -.0526$$

$$EX^2 = \frac{1}{38}(35)^2 + \frac{37}{38}(-1)^2 = \frac{1262}{38} = 33.2, \text{ and}$$

$$p = \frac{1}{2} - \frac{.0526}{2\sqrt{33.2}} = .4954336.$$

However, before we begin to use the conventional gambler's ruin formulas we must also divide the player's initial capital by $\sqrt{EX^2}$. Let's practice the method by approximating a roulette number bettor's chance of doubling a stake of 50 units. As above, we assume p = .4954336 and also that the original stake is a = $50\sqrt{EX^2}$ = 50/5.7629 = 8.6763. Hence p^a = .002257, q^a = .002645, and the chance of doubling is estimated as

$$\frac{.002257}{.002257 + .002645} = .4605.$$

The following table shows how mistaken it is to assume that the roulette player's probability of doubling his capital doesn't depend upon what type of bet he makes. If you have a calculator with an exponential button you might try to verify the entries in the last column, which are approximations to the actual figures just to their left.

Roulette Player's Chance of Doubling Stake

Initial Capital	Chance of doubling with color bet	Chance of doubling with number bet	Approximate chance of doubling with number bet
50	.0051	.4087	.4605
100	.000027	.3936	.4214
200	.000000	.3348	.3466
400	.000000	.2187	.2196
500	.000000	.1716	.1701

Certainly the figures in the second column are of no use in estimating the actual values for doubling capital with a number bet, shown in the third column.

What's also surprising is the persistent chance of the number bettor to double his capital. Although I haven't worked out the precise figures, our approximation suggests the player still has about a 10% chance of doubling a stake of 700 units and a 5% chance of doubling 900 units. This illustrates the general truism that if one is going to play unfavorable games he's better off to gamble as wildly as possible.

(Note, in this regard, that if we changed our hypothesis so the color bettor could bet as many units as he wanted on any coup, rather than just one, he'd always have an 18/38 = 47% chance of doubling his bank, by betting it all, and this would be his best strategy. An intriguing contradiction to this generally optimal policy of betting as much as possible in unfavorable games to achieve a desired level of fortune was discovered by Stewart Ethier for the game of craps with odds. Stewart found a balance between the "bet all" approach and the holding back of some capital to take advantage of the odds, correspondingly reducing, in a sense, the house edge. As a result he was able to raise the seemingly optimal $949/1925 = .493$ chance of doubling $100 with the Don't Pass bet to about .494. His paper appears in the *Journal of Operations Research* for those interested.)

Games With More Than Two Possible Outcomes

Blackjack is even more difficult to analyze in this fashion, and those interested should look at the Appendix to Chapter Nine of my book *The Theory of Blackjack.* As an example of a game with more than two possible outcomes we'll contrive a simple one which will lead to easy arithmetic. Suppose our gambler loses three units 20% of the time, wins two units 50% of the time, loses one unit 20% of the time, and ties the other 10%.

A chart will prove convenient here to calculate both EX, the player's advantage, and EX^2, the player's average squared result.

Possible value	Probability		
X	P(X)	X · P(X)	X^2 · P(X)
−3	.2	−.6	1.8
+2	.5	+1.0	2.0
−1	.2	−.2	.2
0	.1	.0	.0
	1.0	EX = +.2	$EX^2 = 4$

By our formula, we assume the player's single trial probability of success to be

$$p = \frac{1}{2} + \frac{EX}{2\sqrt{EX^2}} = .5 + \frac{.2}{2\sqrt{4}} = .5 + .05 = .55.$$

To find the chance, for instance, of doubling a bank of 20 units we divide this initial capital by

$$\sqrt{EX} = \sqrt{4} = 2$$

and use the standard formula with $p = .55$ and $a = 20/2 = 10$:

$$\frac{(.55)^{10}}{(.45)^{10} + (.55)^{10}} = .8815$$

The precise figure appears in the following table of actual and approximate probabilities of doubling various initial stakes for this game. For larger initial stakes you can see the approximations are quite accurate. Again, you may wish to try to reproduce them with your calculator.

Initial Stake	Actual Chance of Doubling	Approximate Chance of Doubling
1	.5556	.5205
2	.6417	.5500
3	.5705	.5747
4	.6270	.5990
5	.6429	.6229
10	.7419	.7317
20	.8838	.8815
30	.9530	.9530
40	.9818	.9822
50	.9931	.9934

The precise solution to the problem of doubling capital is as suggested, quite difficult by formal mathematics. However, for those with computers there is a simple program to write and to run which will do the job.

Both to give the reader a feeling for the "difference equations" which govern such phenomena and to illustrate the calculations the computer performs to solve such problems, we'll work out the exact chance of doubling an initial bank of two units in this game. We let P(I) stand for the probability of successfully doubling the initial bank, given that the player currently possesses exactly I units. The following equations show the relations among the various values of P(I):

$$P(1) = .1 \times P(1) + .5 \times P(3)$$
$$P(2) = .2 \times P(1) + .1 \times P(2) + .5 \times P(4)$$
$$P(3) = .2 \times P(2) + .1 \times P(3) + .5 \times P(5)$$
$$P(4) = 1$$
$$P(5) = 1$$

The first three equations show how often and whereto the player's fortune must move in order to maintain a chance of ultimately doubling the two unit bank. The last two equations embody the notion that when the player reaches four or five units, he has already succeeded, since his fortune is at least four units. Hence the only unknowns are the first three:

$$P(1) = .1 \times P(1) + .5 \times P(3)$$
$$P(2) = .2 \times P(1) + .1 \times P(2) + .5$$
$$P(3) = .2 \times P(2) + .1 \times P(3) + .5$$

One method of solving such a system of equations involving probabilities is a sort of "trial and error" method called "Gauss-Seidel Iteration". We attempt to determine the unknowns by using these formulas, employing the most previously computed (really approximated) values for the other variables used at each step. Initially we suppose all values to be zero. The first "iteration" gives

$$P(1) = .1 \times 0 + .5 \times 0 = 0$$
$$P(2) = .2 \times 0 + .1 \times 0 + .5 = .5$$
$$P(3) = .2 \times .5 + .1 \times 0 + .5 = .6$$

The second iteration increases P(1) above zero:

$$P(1) = .1 \times 0 + .5 \times .6 = .3$$
$$P(2) = .2 \times .3 + .1 \times .5 + .5 = .61$$
$$P(3) = .2 \times .61 + .1 \times .6 + .5 = .682$$

The third iteration produces:

$$P(1) = .1 \times .3 + .5 \times .682 = .371$$
$$P(2) = .2 \times .371 + .1 \times .61 + .5 = .6352$$
$$P(3) = .2 \times .6352 + .1 \times .682 + .5 = .6952$$

Then

$$P(1) = .1 \times .371 + .5 \times .6952 = .3847$$
$$P(2) = .2 \times .3847 + .1 \times .6352 + .5 = .6405$$
$$P(3) = .2 \times .6405 + .1 \times .6952 + .5 = .6976$$

The next iteration gives P(2) = .6415, and the sixth one P(2) = .6417, accurate to four digits.

In the BASIC language, a program to perform the calculations for doubling a bank of, say, B=20 units would be:

```
 2    DIM P(500)
 4    B=20
 6    M=2*B
 8    P(M)=1
10    P(M+1)=1
15    For I=1 to 100
20    For J=1 to 100
22    P(1)=.1*P(1)+.5*P(3)
24    P(2)=.2*P(1)+.1*P(2)+.5*P(4)
26    P(3)=.2*P(2)+.1*P(3)+.5*P(5)
28    For K=4 to M-1
30    P(K)=.2*P(K-3)+.2*P(K-1)+.1*P(K)+
      .5*P(K+2)
32    Next K
35    Next J
40    Print P(B)
45    Next I
```

Statement 40 is designed to print out the current P(B) = P(20) every 100 iterations, showing us if it has stabilized to its correct value. The program can be stopped then.

Naturally other aspects of gambler's ruin problems are also approximable by this method. For example, suppose in the previous game the player refused to stop after doubling his capital of 20 units and instead chose to gamble on until he was either ruined or became infinitely wealthy. We could estimate his chance of ruin by using the formula

$$\left(\frac{q}{p}\right)^a \text{ with } q - .45, p = .55, \text{ and } a = \frac{20}{\sqrt{EX^2}} = 10,$$

81

obtaining $\left(\dfrac{.45}{.55}\right)^{10} = .1344.$

Similarly our estimate of his chance of never falling behind would be $y = 2 - 1/p = .1818$ while our estimate of his chance of always being ahead, which is also his long run chance of being at a new all time high, becomes $x = 2p - 1 = .1000.$

Again, Gauss-Seidel Iteration can be used to find the actual values to any desired degree of accuracy. Let $Q(I)$ be the chance of ultimate ruin in this game, given that the player currently has I units and is determined to gamble forever or until ruin:

```
 2   DIM Q(500)
 4   M=200
 6   Q(0)=1
 8   For I=1 to 100
10   For J=1 to 100
12   Q(1)=.4+.1*Q(1)+.5*Q(3)
14   Q(2)=.2+.2*Q(1)+.1*Q(2)+.5*Q(4)
16   For K=3 to M-1
18   Q(K)=.2*Q(K-3) + .2*Q(K-1)+
     .1*Q(K) +.5*Q(K+2)
20   Next K
22   Next J
24   Print Q(2), Q(20)
26   Next I
```

What we do here is introduce a level of wealth M (tentatively 200 in this program) at which we assume there is essentially no chance of ultimate ruin. Run the program for increasing values of M until there is no change in the computed ruin probabilities, and that should be it. (Since Q(M) is approximately $(.45/.55)^{m/2}$, it would be effectively zero for large enough M; example: $(.45/.55)^{100} = .00000002$.) We learn Q(20) = .1319 (compare with the approximate .1344) and Q(2) = .7612. The latter can be used to find the actual value of x, the chance of always being ahead after the first coup: $x = .5 \times (1 - Q(2))$, since the player necessarily must win the first coup and then never be ruined thereafter. Hence the true value of x is $.5 \times (1 - .7612) = .1194$ (compare to .1000).

The actual chance of never being behind, y, can also be found from a similar program, the details of which we leave up to the reader. It is y = .1612 (compare the approximate .1818).

Note that the true values of x and y, .1194 and .1612, are considerably closer together than their surrogate approximations of .1000 and .1818, which are based upon the assumption of winning or losing exactly one unit on each play. We can come up with an explanation for this if we recall, from the previous article, the interpretation of y − x as the long run probability of being currently at an all time high that had been visited before.

The most likely way to revisit an all time high when the game has payoffs of just +1 and −1 is to be at it, then to lose the next game, and then to immediately win back the lost ground again. With p = .55 the chance of this sort of quick return to an all time high two steps later is $(1 - p) \times p = .2475$, which is rather considerable. But in our actual gamble, if one is at an all time high and then experiences a loss followed by an

83

immediate win, he does not return to the previous high. He will be either one unit below it or one unit above it, in which latter case he would then be establishing a brand new all time high. We should note that there is a partially compensating increase in the chance of revisiting an all time high, namely by achieving a payoff of zero (a tie) and merely staying at the previous high. This happens with a probability of .1 in the game we are studying. Overall, however, revisits to an all time high are less likely in the actual gamble than in its approximate idealization as a game in which we win or lose one unit at each stage.

10

OPTIMAL WAGERS ON SIMULTANEOUS BETS

Having picked the wrong team in all five 1982 New Years' Day bowl games, it seems natural for me to turn my attention to writing a critique of the proportional betting advice in the December 30, 1981 issue #17 of HIGH ROLLER, an $8 publication devoted to sports prognostication. That way, A.E. Housman's caustic commentary on an unfavored colleague, "There's no telling on what subject he may next display his versatile incapacity," will be doubly pertinent: to me for trying to predict football and to HIGH ROLLER for presuming to analyze the mathematics of proportional betting.

Briefly, a proportional, or fixed fraction, betting scheme is designed for gamblers playing favorable games. In order to maximize long term growth potential the gambler should wager a fraction of his capital that depends upon his advantage for the next bet. The problem is to determine the optimal, or best, fraction. Readers interested in more background as well as a useful bibliography on the subject should consult Joel Friedman's paper *Understanding and Applying the Kelly Criterion*, presented to the Fifth National Conference on Gambling, sponsored by the Department of Economics of the University of Nevada at Reno.

It is well known that for wagering on repeated and independent trials of a game for which the gambler has probability p of winning one unit and $q = 1 - p$ of losing a unit, the optimal fraction of capital to wager is $p - q$ which is also the gambler's expectation per play. Then after each outcome the gambler recalculates his optimal wager as the fraction $p - q$ times his new and current bankroll.

HIGH ROLLER treats the dilemma of a football prognosticator who must make several simultaneous wagers on a given Saturday or Sunday and thus is denied the luxury of recalculating his optimal wager after each play since the bets on some games must be made before the results of previous ones are known. HIGH ROLLER suggests that when making n independent wagers the best strategy is to make each bet equal to the player's correct Kelly Criterion bet for a single wager divided by the square root of n to account for the uncertainty associated with not knowing the outcomes of the simultaneous wagers.

I shall show that this is not the result decreed by the canons of mathematics. First we idealize that each wager has the same probability p of being successful, although I personally regard this as the most dubious aspect of the analysis for sports betting. I maintain this skepticism for two reasons, one being that it seems unlikely for even the successful prognosticator to have the same probability of success under all circumstances, the other based on this value of p usually being an estimate arrived at using last year's data, the very data which probably suggested the method of prediction! Nevertheless, since the assumption of equal success probabilities is HIGH ROLLER'S, we'll use it for purposes of illustration.

As HIGH ROLLER doesn't make it clear whether the bookie vigorish (eleven is wagered to win ten) has been taken into account, we must distinguish two cases. First we assume that each of n independent, simultaneous, wagers wins or loses one unit, with the same probability p of winning. In this case the optimal fraction, f, is given very nearly by

$$f = \frac{p - q}{4pq + n(p - q)^2} \; .$$

This equation is exact for n = 1 and n = 2 but only approximate for larger values. The exact solution for n = 3 wagers is the solution to the cubic equation

$$3f^3 - (p - q)(1 + 8pq)f^2 - (3 - 8pq)f + (p - q) = 0$$

and for larger values of n the precise determination gets out of hand very rapidly, it requiring the solution to an nth degree equation.

The following numerical example will provide a comparison of this approximation, the exact solution, and HIGH ROLLER'S recommendation. We'll use p = .54 and q = 1 − .54 = .46 to create a gamble with an 8% advantage as HIGH ROLLER hypothesizes in its article.

n	Approximation	Exact Solution	HIGH ROLLER'S Recommendation
1	.08	.08	.08
2	.079491	.079491	.056569
3	.078989	.078976	.046188
4	.0785	.0783	.0400
10	.0756	.0751	.0253
14	.0739	.0709	.0214

There is a sound intuitive reason for the proper fractions not to differ very much from the value of .08, appropriate for sequentially made non-simultaneous wagers. For example, suppose the unlikely worst case that we knew we'd lost our first three wagers. Then our fourth bet would be for 8% of our new capital, which would be $(.92)^3 = .7787$ of our original bank: $.08(.7787) = .0623$ which is still far above HIGH ROLLER'S recommended .04.

To take into account the bookie vigorish on eleven to ten bets, the following approximation can be used. Again, n simultaneous bets each have probability p of being successful, although the successes only yield 10/11 of the amount risked. The best fraction f is nearly

$$\frac{11\left(21p-11\right)}{441\,pq + n\left(21p-11\right)^2}.$$

The exact solution for n = 1 is

$$f = \frac{21p-11}{10}$$

which is of course simpler to implement than the approximation. With n = 2, however, things get more complicated and the precise solution would come from the quadratic equation:

$$20 f^2 + \left(420\, p - 441\ p^2 - 209\right)f + \left(231\ p - 121\right) = 0.$$

To create a numerical illustration having 8% gambler advantage on any bet we need to solve

$$\frac{10\, p}{11} - q = .08 \text{ for p.}$$

Substituting q = 1 – p, we quickly find

$$p = \frac{11.88}{21} = .565714$$

is the required ability to predict and q = 1 – p = .434286. Now our comparison chart becomes

n	Approximation	Exact Solution	HIGH ROLLER'S Recommendation
1	.0887	.0880	.0880
2	.0881	.0874	.0622
3	.0875	.0867	.0508
4	.0869	.0860	.0440
10	.0834	.0818	.0278
14	.0812	.07137	.0235

It should be noted that both my approximation and HIGH ROLLER'S recommendation could occasionally suggest betting more money than one possesses if n is very large. If n is greater than 13 for the two numerical examples considered, my approximation suggests betting more than the entire bankroll and yet this is not really too misleading for, with more than 13 such favorable bets, the exactly optimal strategy is to bet *almost* all of the bankroll anyway. For example, making 14 bets of .0709 of one's bankroll as in the first case uses 14 × .0709 = .993 of the bankroll, while in the second 14 × .07137 = .999.

The approximation I recommend is based on the optimal Kelly fraction being approximately the expected win from the gamble divided by the average squared result. This estimate is generally quite good when the player's advantage is small, regardless of the nature of the possible outcomes. Such is generally the case in the game of blackjack.

One of the recurrent questions about optimal wagering in the game of blackjack involves how much to bet when playing more than one hand at the same table, and the previous principle provides an answer. If you are using the Kelly Criterion in blackjack, bet the fraction $2/(n + 1.6)$ times your advantage on each of n simultaneous hands. For example, with a 5% advantage, the proper fractions would be

n = Number of hands	Fraction on each hand	Total Expectation
1	3.8%	.19%
2	2.8%	.28%
3	2.2%	.33%
4	1.8%	.36%
5	1.5%	.38%
6	1.3%	.39%
7	1.2%	.41%

The advantage of taking extra hands is seen in the right hand "Total Expectation" column – we expect to win more money, but with the same amount of risk to our bankroll. There are practical considerations of course: there are not always extra spots on the table available and the extra cards used by the extra hands may result in fewer rounds being dealt from a favorable deck or shoe.

The figure $2/(n + 1.6)$ can be justified by observing that playing n hands has two principal effects:

a) it multiplies the expected gain by a factor of n, and
b) it raises the variance of one blackjack hand from approximately 1.3 squared units to about $n(1.3) + n(n - 1)/2$.

Effect b) comes from an analysis which suggests that the covariance of two simultaneous hands is about 1/2. Since the variance is very nearly the average squared result, we divide the n of a) by the $n(1.3) + n(n - 1)/2$ of b) to get our appropriate fraction.

Next time we'll discuss some interesting problems in probability whose solutions involve "transcendental" numbers. Between now and then you might carry out a couple of experiments.

First, rule a very large piece of paper with parallel horizontal lines whose distance apart is precisely the length of a toothpick (or needle). Then drop the toothpick on the ruled paper from a point as high above the paper as is practical. Record how often the toothpick crosses one of the horizontal lines.

Second, the next time you have two dollars check the last three digits of the serial number. Do these numbers have any common divisors? For example, my bills are L768001*119*I and L51168*057*J. My three digit numbers are 119 and 57. 119 factors into 7 × 17 and 57 factors into 3 × 19, so my pair has no common divisor. Numbers with no common divisor are called "relatively prime." What is the chance of this?

Or, try this with dollars. How many dollars do you need so that the sum of these last three digits exceeds 1000? For my dollars above, the sum is 119+57=176 so I pull out another dollar. L06882*398*J gives 176+398=574. Finally my fourth dollar, L29140*872*J, gives 574+872=1446 which is greater than 1000. Two is the minimal number necessary; what is the average number required to get the total of the last three digits greater than 1000?

11

TRANSCENDENTAL PROBABILITIES

In my last article I invited the reader to carry out a few experiments. The first involved dropping a needle or toothpick onto a piece of paper ruled with parallel lines whose distances apart were the same as the length of the object dropped. (In fact a toothpick is preferable since its greater air resistance imparts a fluttering propeller-like effect which makes its orientation upon landing more random.) On this page is an illustration of the ten results I got when I performed the experiment.

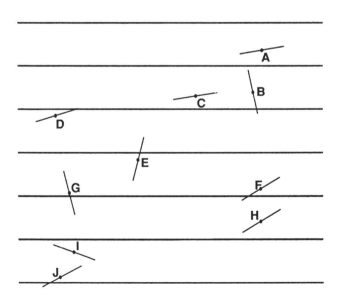

What we're interested in is how often the toothpick crosses, or touches, one of the horizontal grid lines. As you can see in my experiment this happened six times, in cases B, D, E, F, G, and J. In mathematics this is called the Buffon needle problem, named after a Count Buffon who first proposed it. What's interesting is that the long run probability (after many trials) that the needle or toothpick crosses one of the grid lines is $2/\pi$ = .6366...where $\pi = 3.1416...$is the ratio of the circumference of a circle to its diameter, encountered in high school geometry.

$2/\pi$ is a strange probability to most of us, accustomed as we are to fractions whose numerator and denominator are both whole numbers, the whole numbers usually being the number of successful outcomes for an event and the total number of possibilities. π is a peculiar denominator in that it is neither a whole number nor a quotient of whole numbers (called a "rational" number).

Let's take a look at two more probability problems, one geometric and the other decidedly not, whose solutions involve this marvelous number π which has intrigued mankind for several thousand years. On the next page are located 17 dots, representing 17 tiny seeds which I dropped upon a piece of paper of similar proportion to the page.

What we're concerned with here is the notion of "nearest neighbor." That is, what dot is closest to, for instance, dot A? As we can see it is C, and hence we term C "A's nearest neighbor." Now, who is C's nearest neighbor? In particular, is it A, and are A and C "mutual nearest neighbors" in that they are the nearest neighbor of their nearest neighbors? The answer is obviously no since C's nearest neighbor is D.

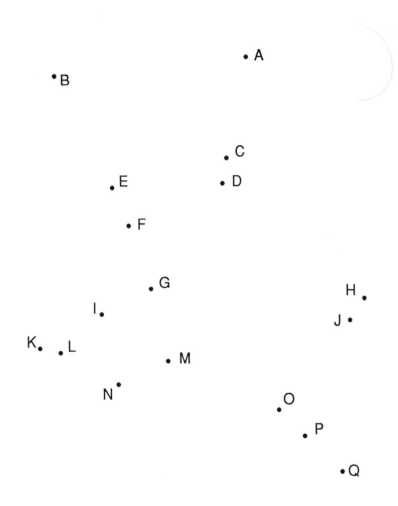

But behold, D's nearest neighbor *is* C and so C and D *are* mutual nearest neighbors. Similarly we find E and F, H and J, K and L, N and M, and O and P are pairs of mutual nearest neighbors, while A, B, G, I, and Q do not have this property. Hence $12/17 = .706$ is the empirical probability, in *this* experiment, that a dot will be the nearest neighbor of its nearest neighbor.

It can be proven that for a very large number of randomly distributed dots the probability is

$$\frac{1}{\frac{4}{3} + \frac{\sqrt{3}}{2\pi}} = .6215 \ldots$$

that any particular dot will be in such a mutual nearest neighbor relation with some other dot. This probability is interesting in that it not only involves π, but also $\sqrt{3}$ which cannot be expressed as a quotient of two whole numbers. Both π and $\sqrt{3}$ are termed "irrational" numbers because of this, but there is a further classification of irrational numbers which distinguishes them and puts π in a very interesting category of what are called "transcendental" numbers.

While it is true that $\sqrt{3}$ cannot be expressed as the quotient of two whole numbers (and hence is termed irrational), it is also true that $\sqrt{3}$ is a solution to a polynomial equation within which all the coefficients are whole numbers: $x^2 - 3 = 0$ has $\sqrt{3}$ as a solution. On the contrary it has been proven that π is not the solution of any such polynomial equation with whole number coefficients and for that reason π is termed a *transcendental* number. In a sense transcendental numbers have a higher order of mystery surrounding them than algebraic, albeit irrational, numbers like $\sqrt{3}$.

To create a non-geometric probability problem in which the transcendental π plays a role, we'll look at the last three digits of the serial numbers of two dollar bills. For our purposes we'll refer to these last three digits as the serial number, unless all three digits are zeros in which case we'll call the serial number 1000, in order to avoid zero itself. What we're doing is using the dollar bills as a source of random numbers between one and 1000.

Now, the original serial numbers of my two dollars are B54453604K and L17699437A. Hence I use 604 and 437 as my two numbers, and what I'm concerned with is whether these two numbers have any proper divisors in common. $604 = 2 \times 2 \times 151$ with all of the factors being *prime* (i.e., unfactorable) and $437 = 19 \times 23$. Hence my two dollars have no divisors in common and are consequently called "relatively prime."

What is the probability that any two numbers randomly selected from one to 1000 will be relatively prime? It takes the computer less than ten seconds to determine the chance to be .608383.

Another way to do this is by using birthdays rather than serial numbers of dollar bills. Here's how. Let us redescribe every birthday by what *day of the year* it is, rather than with the traditional reference to month and then day of the month. Then, if we exclude the few unfortunates born on February 29, we have a source of random numbers from one to 365. For example, my birthday is July 19, the 200th day of the year, Stanford Wong's birthday is April 3, the 93rd day of the year, and Ed Thorp's August 14th translates into 226.

Factoring these three numbers, we get

GRIFFIN $200 = 2 \times 2 \times 2 \times 5 \times 5$
WONG $93 = 3 \times 31$
THORP $226 = 2 \times 113$

Of the three possible pairs of individuals we have, we see that 2/3 of the birthday pairs (those which include Wong) are relatively prime. A computer (much more quickly than before, in less than five seconds) determines that the probability that two random birthdays are relatively prime is .609908.

Now, what is the promised role that π plays in all of this? Well, if we let our interval on which we're selecting random number pairs grow longer and longer, say from one to 1,000,000 and beyond, it has been proven (See Christopher, *On the Asymptotic Density of Some k-dimensional Sets;* AMM, Vol. LXIII, 1956.) that the probability the two numbers are relatively prime will approach $6/\pi^2 = .607927$. Note our results for 365 and 1000 are already quite close to this limiting figure, and if we looked at all number pairs selected from one to 100,000 we'd get .607930.

Quickly now, before reading on, guess what the chance of 50 heads occurring in 100 tosses of a coin is. It wouldn't surprise me if many readers give the most common guess of 50%. Undoubtedly, many people are influenced by the

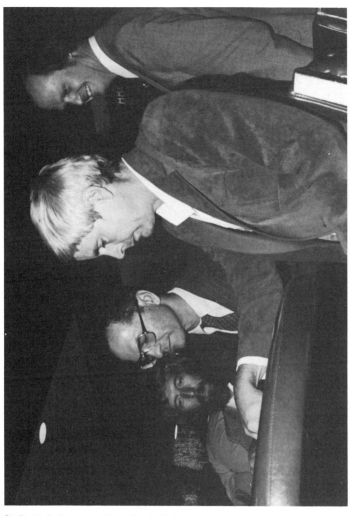

Birthday Boys - Classic assemblage of perhaps the three greatest names in blackjack. From left: Stanford Wong, Edward Thorp and Peter Griffin. William Eadington looks on. Picture was taken at a blackjack table at Barney's Casino (now Bill's) during the Fifth National Conference on Gambling and Risk Taking held in 1981 at Lake Tahoe.

99

similarity of the 50 out of 100 heads to the 50% that they know to be the chance of a head on a single toss. The precise probability is quite an arithmetic tour de force to work out, but it can be very well approximated by the following rule:

The probability of exactly n heads in 2n tosses of a fair coin (the "break-even" number) is approximately $1/\sqrt{n\pi}$.

The following chart shows just how well the approximation works.

n = Number of heads	Exact probability in 2n tosses	Approximation $1/\sqrt{n\pi}$
1	.5	.5642
2	.375	.3989
10	.1762	.1784
50	.0796	.0798
5000	.0080	.0080

This tidbit was imparted to me by Tom Cover of Stanford University at the Monte Carlo Casino bar in Reno in 1974, following an American Mathematical Society session on gambling. I still have the cocktail napkin on which he wrote it and its justification. Believe it or not, I actually had occasion (as the lawyers say) to use it in a court deposition I was giving: an attorney for the U.S. Playing Card Co. asked me if I knew what the chance of getting 5,000 heads in 10,000 tosses of a coin was. Thanks to Tom Cover, I was able to tell him without much delay!

π is by no means the only transcendental number, and there's another equally famous and important one coming up. Toward this end consider the problem of how many people you would need so that the sum of their birthdays (described in the previous sense as numbers from one to 365) first exceeded 365.

As an example let's take the birthdays of Griffin, Wong, and Thorp, in that order. Obviously my birthday, by itself, cannot be greater than 365, so we add Wong's getting 200 + 93 = 293. Hence at least one more is necessary. Thorp's 226, the third birthday, gives us 200 + 93 + 226 = 519 which is greater than 365. So in this case, with this order, it required three birthdays.

Looking at the 3! = 6 possible orders the birthdays could appear in, we see that twice we were able to get the required total with only two birthdays while the other four times we required all three.

Order	Number required to total over 365	How achieved
GWT	3	200 + 93 + 226
GTW	2	200 + 226
WGT	3	93 + 200 + 226
WTG	3	93 + 226 + 200
TGW	2	226 + 200
TWG	3	226 + 93 + 200
Total	16	Average = 16/6 = 2.67

For these three individuals the average number of birthdays required to create a total exceeding 365 was 16/6 = 2.67.

Of course, it would sometimes require four, or even more people, especially if there were many January birthdays. What's interesting is that the average number of people required, considering all possible birthdays equally likely, is $(366/365)^{365} = 2.71457$ and this is very nearly the important mathematical constant $\mathbf{e} = 2.71828...$

(At a recent seminar sponsored by the Albertan Gaming Control Board in Calgary, I went around the room asking all the participants their birthdays until the total was greater than 365. Then I began again. The result was that nine times it took two people, once it required four people, and there were two occasions each for both three people and five people. To summarize, I completed a total greater than 365 fourteen times, using 38 people. $38/14 = 2.71429$, my sample average, is remarkably close to the ideal figure of 2.71457. Another interesting occurrence was a triplication of birthdays. July 19 was shared by me and two others.)

We could perform the same sort of experiment with the three digit serial numbers of dollar bills mentioned previously. In this case we would keep selecting new dollars and adding their serial numbers (the last three digits, as we agreed) until the total first exceeded 1000. The average number of dollar bills necessary to achieve this will be $(1001/1000)^{1000} = 2.71692$ which is even closer to the famous number $\mathbf{e}$.

(If we are sampling repeatedly and independently from the collection of equally likely integers $\{1,2,3,...N\}$, adding each observation consecutively until the cumulative total first exceeds n ≤ N, then the expected, or average, number of observations required is:

$$E_n = \left(1 + \frac{1}{N}\right)^n$$

This can be easily proved by induction from the obvious relation:

$$E_{n+1} = 1 + \frac{1}{N} \sum_{j=0}^{n} E_j$$

The gratuitous use of modifiers such as "easily" and "obvious" is frequently favored by mathematicians desirous of suggesting their superiority to readers who, less familiar with the subject, may have to puzzle at some length on the matter.)

One can imagine a gambling game on this basis: put many dollars into an opaque container and have the gambler pay the casino, say, $2.75 for the right to select bills until the total of the serial numbers exceeds 1000 for the first time. The gambler keeps all the bills up to and including the last one. On the average he gets back about $2.72, leaving the house with a small vigorish of 3¢.

Before we examine another matter where the number **e** plays an important probabilistic role, let's take a look at **e**'s origin. Just as π had a geometric interpretation (as the ratio of the circumference of a circle to the diameter) so too can we invent, or contrive, **e** in the context of a graph or picture.

You may recall from a previous issue of *C&S* the graph of the curve y = 1/x. When x = 1, y = 1; when x = 2, y = 1/2; when x = 3, y = 1/3; etc. **e** happens to be the number, along the x-axis, such that the area underneath the curve y = 1/x between 1 and **e** is precisely one unit, the same area as the illustrated square built upon the line segment from x = 0 to x = 1.

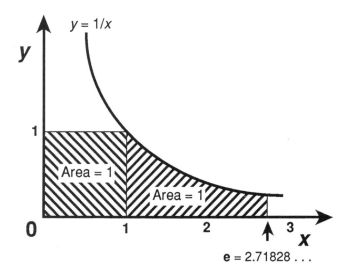

Just as π's role in probability is not confined to just one case, the same is true of **e**. One of its more interesting manifestations arises in the famous "matching hats" problem. Imagine several inebriates retrieve at random their hats, previously stored in the cloakroom before the party began. What is the chance that no man gets his own hat back? For instance, with n = 4 men there are 4! = 4 × 3 × 2 × 1 = 24 ways to redistribute their hats at random, nine of which result in no man getting his own hat back:

Men	Redistributions with no man getting his own hat								
A	B	B	B	C	C	C	D	D	D
B	A	D	C	A	D	D	A	C	C
C	D	A	D	D	A	B	B	A	B
D	C	C	A	B	B	A	C	B	A

Redistribution with at least one man getting his own hat

A	A	A	A	A	A	A	B	B	B	C	C	C	D	D	D
B	B	B	C	C	D	D	A	C	D	A	B	B	A	B	B
C	C	D	B	D	B	C	C	A	C	B	A	D	C	A	C
D	D	C	D	B	C	B	D	D	A	D	D	A	B	C	A

The remarkable thing about this problem is that most people, when asked to guess what the chance of no man getting his own hat back would be for a very large number of men (like n=1000), would make a guess either very close to one (reflecting certainty) or close to zero (impossibility). And yet the answer stabilizes, for even modestly sized values of n, near .36787944 = 1/e, the reciprocal of our new found friend **e**. There is an interesting pattern to the probabilities for various values of n:

P[no hat back among n men] =

P[no hat back among n − 1 men] + $(-1)^n/n!$

Number of men n	n!	$(-1)^n/n!$	P[no men gets his own hat back among n men]
1	1		0/1 = .000000
2	2	$+1/2$	1/2 = .500000
3	6	$-1/6$	2/6 = .333333
4	24	$+1/24$	9/24 = .375000
5	120	$-1/120$	44/120 = .366667
6	720	$+1/720$	265/720 = .368056
7	5040	$-1/5040$	1854/5040 = .367857
8	40320	$+1/40320$	14833/40320 = .367882
9	362880	$-1/362880$	133496/362880 = .367879
10	3628800	$+1/3628800$	1334961/3628800 = .36787946

You can simulate this event yourself. Take the ace, two,...through ten of some suit out of a deck of cards. Then, after shuffling thoroughly your ten cards, turn them over one at a time while counting aloud the numbers one to ten. If the number you're calling matches the card you turn, quit and record a failure. Otherwise try to get through all ten cards with no match. If you do, record a success. The relative frequency of your successes to your total trials should approach $1/e$, and it will if you have *patience*.

Next time we'll discuss different ways of measuring the gambler's (or casino's) win rate and show how failure to specify the method may lead to confusion and disagreement. We'll examine the controversy caused by the ECON report on card counting to the New Jersey Casino Control Commission and I'll present a dice betting system which only requires 31 dollars to capitalize it and will yield an average win rate above 56%!

12

DIFFERENT WAYS TO DESCRIBE
WIN RATE (OR PC)

The origin of many disagreements is the failure of the contending parties to specify what it is they are arguing about. Often two people will use the same words without realizing that they each have different understandings of the words' meanings. Such disputes, of course, cannot be reconciled until common agreement is reached on terminology.

Hold Percentage

Mathematicians frequently confuse, and are confused by, casino personnel in discussions of win rate (or %) for a game like roulette. The mathematician describes the house advantage as 5.26% for a color bet in roulette because for every 38 units wagered the house *expects* to win a net of $20 - 18 = 2$ units since there are 20 ways for it to win and only 18 ways for the player. $2/38 = .0526 = 5.26\%$ is then the expected gain *per bet made* and is the "mathematical percentage."

Casino bosses have, however, evolved a different method of describing the performance of, for instance, a roulette table. They might say that "The PC in roulette is 20%" or "The roulette table holds 20%." This figure is an empirical one necessitated by the type of bookkeeping casinos use to monitor performance and appears greatly at variance with the mathematicians' 5%. Who's correct?

Well, a better question is "How is the 20% hold figure in roulette arrived at?" To illustrate the casino point of view we'll start with the simplest possible example: one roulette table and only one gambler. Suppose the player buys in for $100 worth of chips and plays for exactly one hour. He may occasionally be ahead or possibly be wiped out within that hour, but let's imagine he terminates his play (either of his own desire or because the casino closes the table) with $80 worth of chips which he takes to the cashier to be redeemed in money. The pit boss analyzes the table's performance by comparing the $100 drop in the cash box with the 80 missing chips in the money tray. The difference, $100 - 80 = 20$, is the amount that this table "held" and the quotient of "hold" divided by "drop" or $20/100 = 20\%$, is the casino's **hold percentage**.

It's important to realize that hold percentage is an empirical, even to some extent sociological, figure. It varies from day to day, year to year, and especially it varies with the characteristics of the players. The problem is greatly complicated when there are different ways to play a game such as craps which have different *mathematical* percentages and when players, as they frequently do, carry chips from table to table or game to game.

A couple of oversimplified examples may help to illustrate this dependence. First, suppose our previously described solitary gambler has enormous endurance and is determined to play forever or until he loses his entire $100 buy in. Since roulette is an unfavorable game this latter eventuality is the assured result. However long it takes, when our indefatigable gambler has finally lost all his money and the casino closes the table it will be discovered that all of the chips are still there *and* so too is the hundred dollar bill in the drop box. Hence the casino won 100% of the drop. A mathematician keeping score would count the, perhaps, 1900 dollar bets the gambler made and report the casino win rate as 100/1900 = 5.26%.

Now let's introduce another table and another gambler. Mr. A buys in for $100 at table #1, plays for awhile, and then walks away a net loser of $20. Mr. B buys in at table #2 for just one dollar, wins a dollar, and walks to the cashier a net winner. Now Mr. A walks over to table #2 with the 80 chips *he bought at table #1*. He plays for an hour and only loses two chips at table #2. How will the casino hold performance look for the two tables? As in the very first example, table #1 will show a 20/100 = 20% win rate. But what about table #2? Mr. B took away two chips, the one he bought and the one he won; Mr. A left two chips, the ones he lost. Hence the table has as many chips as it started with and concludes it "held" all of the drop (Mr. B's drop incidentally, and he was a winner!), or 100%.

As insusceptible as win/drop is to precise mathematical prediction it does nevertheless remain a useful method of description for casinos. The empirical percentages derive a long term validity because of the large flow of action.

Perhaps one exception to this is the game of blackjack where education of the players has probably reduced the casino hold percent over the years, although not the profits which continue to grow because of increased volume.

Throwing Out Ties

Another common source of disagreement which occurs even among mathematicians was highlighted for me by a conversation with the manager of a prospering Las Vegas casino. He quoted a 1.37% mathematical advantage for the Player bet in baccarat. This grated against my memory of a 1.24% edge for the house and I demurred. It didn't occur to me until later that we both could be considered correct *providing* that we specified whether we meant percentage advantage per *resolved* bet (the 1.37%) or per hand *dealt* (the 1.24%).

The disagreement is quickly resolved by looking at 10,000 baccarat hands broken down into the ideal categories of 4586 Bank wins, 4462 Player wins, and 952 ties. My 1.24% comes from the 4586 – 4462 = 124 units net loss on the Player bet divided by the 10,000 hands played. The 1.37% arises from dividing this 124 unit loss by 9048, the number of hands which *don't* result in a tie.

I touched on this point in my first article for *C&S* in which the 1980 ideal results for the Don't Pass bet in craps were categorized as 949 winning bets, 976 losers, and 55 standoffs from the bar. The net loss is 27 units which can be summarized either as a 27/1980 = 1.36% loss per *hand* of craps or 27/1925 = 1.40% loss per *resolved* bet.

There is no common agreement even among mathematicians about which description is preferable. Professor Stewart Ethier (then at Michigan State University, now at University of Utah) presented an elaborate mathematical argument for throwing out the ties in his paper *On the House Advantage* presented at the Fifth Conference on Gambling sponsored by the University of Nevada, Reno at Caesars Tahoe in October of 1981. I tend to disagree with Stew on this, preferring average win per hand played, regardless of ties, on the grounds that the player is not compelled to leave his bet out after a tie occurs: when a bet on baccarat or on the Don't Pass line in craps is made we have no guarantee it will be left until resolution of either victory or defeat.

Disagreements on
Blackjack Percentage

Blackjack played according to the basic strategy (best strategy without card counting) is unique in that you don't know ahead of time precisely how much money will be risked on the hand, this because of the possibility of double downs and pair splits. Partially because of this Chambliss and Roginski in *Playing Blackjack in Atlantic City* quoted a lower player expectation for the original Atlantic City blackjack rules than I came up with. Their point of view was that the basic strategist's expected gain should be divided not by his original unit bet, but rather by the average amount of money risked. This latter figure, their divisor, would be about 1.1 times the original amount put in the betting square since, roughly speaking, the player will put out an extra chip on double downs or splits about 10% of the time.

111

I personally favor quoting the average return on the one unit originally put in the betting square on the grounds that it is the realistic measure of how much the player's fortune will *change* as the result of a single blackjack hand. That is, before the hand is dealt we don't know whether we will have to put up any "extra" (doubling or splitting) money or not, but what we do know, the act we can control with certainty, is how much we will put in the betting square. I feel it more useful to describe the player's expected gain or loss relative to this deliberate bet, rather than to some average possible commitment on the hand.

Regardless of which approach one favors, it is interesting to contemplate that the two could lead to different definitions of basic strategy, at least under certain sets of rules. An example which comes to mind arises in the Las Vegas Strip standard single deck game. The player's expectation is precisely +.04% if he uses the correct composition-dependent basic strategy. Now, consider the hand of (A8), or soft 19, against a dealer's six showing. If it is played by standing, the expectation is 48.24%. However, doubling down gives an expectation of 48.26% of the original bet and by my definition doubling down is the proper basic strategy play because it increases expected profit on the hand. The Chambliss-Roginski perspective would presumably rule out doubling down because it must decrease the player's average gain per average unit wagered. We can tell this without elaborate calculation since the marginal gain in player expectation for the extra unit put out on the double down is 48.26% − 48.24% = .02% and this is less than the overall player expectation of .04%.

Paradoxically, if these rules were altered in a fashion completely unrelated to the holding of (A8) v. six the Chambliss-Roginski perspective could change and dictate doubling down the hand. For example, if the blackjack bonus for the player were eliminated the player's expectation would become negative, indeed very negative, at .04% − 2.32% = −2.28%. Now the marginal increase of .02% for the double down dollar would have to improve (albeit minusculely) the player's expected return per average amount risked. I point to this contrived contradiction as an argument in favor of my preference for expected gain per original unit bet.

Uston vs. ECON

Another, highly publicized, disagreement about win rates occurred in June of 1981 during New Jersey's hearings on the elimination of its early surrender rule from blackjack. Ken Uston, a well known blackjack litigant and advocate of maintaining the early surrender rule, called me one day with a request that I offer an opinion to the New Jersey Gaming Control Commission contradicting what he felt to be a very unreasonable aspect of a study presented to the commission by ECON, a consulting firm then under contract to the Atlantic City Resorts Association. When Ken told me that ECON claimed card counters had a win rate of 4.38% my first reaction was to ask him if this could possibly be a win rate of 4.38% of the minimum bet per hand rather than 4.38% of the average amount of money wagered, which latter figure I agreed was way out of line. Ken felt quite certain that their intent was to describe the latter and sent me a copy of the report.

To clarify the distinction, imagine that a blackjack card counter has a 2% advantage half the time and bets nine units. The other half of the time he has a 2% disadvantage and bets only one unit. His average profit per hand will be $1/2 \times 9$ units $\times 2\% - 1/2 \times 1$ unit $\times 2\% = 8\%$ of the minimum betting unit *per hand*. Since his average bet is $1/2 \times 9 + 1/2 \times 1 = 5$ units, this could also be described as a win rate (in percent rather than in betting units) of 8% of a unit divided by the average bet of five units = 1.6% on money invested.

The 1.6% is analogous to what Uston thought ECON's interpretation was while the 8% of minimum betting unit per hand parallels the interpretation I thought was the only justifiable one. When I received a copy of the report from Ken I had to agree that the juxtaposition of the 4.38% in a table with other win rates of players whose scale of wagering was not defined certainly left the impression that ECON's intent was to quote an average win per average bet, as Ken claimed, and which would give a very exaggerated impression of the rate at which card counters could win.

Sometime later, when I discussed the matter with ECON, further questioning elicited that percent of minimum bet per hand had indeed been their intent. The charts in the report were then relabeled for presentation to the Fifth National Conference on Gambling. Since the early surrender rule had already been removed, at least partially on the basis of the earlier version of the report, it is, I think, the view of Ken and many others that the "damage had already been done." Another brouhaha resulting from failure to specify terminology.

114

My Craps System With an
Average Win Rate of 56%

Would you be interested in a craps betting system which has a guaranteed **average win rate** of 56% per application? It sounds too good to be true and if you suspect that the advertised description is misleading you're correct.

My system is nothing more than the old "double up if you lose martingale," starting with 31 units and with the goal of winning one unit. We know very well that this system is a losing one, but let's see how the deceptive description "average win rate of 56%" is indeed justifiable, although not really an accurate measure of the system's worth.

Using a single game winning probability of 976/1980 = .4929, we can compute the ideal distribution of 10,000 players using this double up until you win system with a maximum of five losses because of the initial capitalization of 31 betting units:

Sequence	Frequency	Result	Amount Bet	Win Rate	
W	4929	+1	1	1/1 =	100%
LW	2500	+1	3	1/3 =	33%
LLW	1267	+1	7	1/7 =	14%
LLLW	643	+1	15	1/15 =	7%
LLLLW	326	+1	31	1/31 =	3%
LLLLL	335	−31	31	−31/31 =	−100%
Total	10,000	−720	51,434		

In the last row we see that the 10,000 gamblers *lost* a total of 720 units since 335 lost their entire

115

31 unit stake while the other 9665 won exactly one unit. Further, by multiplying the numbers in the Frequency column by their correspondents in Amount Bet, we come up with the fact that a grand total of 51,434 units was wagered. The 720 unit loss divided by the 51,434 units bet gives us, as it should, the known house advantage in craps of 1.4%.

Where, then, is the advertised 56% win rate? We already know the monetary result for our 10,000 ideal martingale gamblers. If we marched them in one side of a casino and then received their reports when they exited on the other we'd learn that 9665 of them won their one unit while 335 of them lost the entire bankroll of 31. Of those who won, the amounts bet ranged from one to 31 units, and so we would learn of the 720 unit loss and the 51,434 units they all together put into action.

But suppose we solicit different information? When they leave the casino we ask them each to write on a piece of paper their individual win rates, the figures which appear in the last column of our table. If we take the 10,000 pieces of paper and average the numbers on them we come up with the astounding figure of an **average win rate** of +56.5%. And this for a losing system!

The fallacy, if you will, of regarding this 56.5% as a meaningful measure of win rate is that it fails to take into account how much money flowed at the various possible win rates. The mathematical edge of 1.4% we confirmed earlier is really an average win divided by an average bet. It is this latter figure which mathematicians have assured us is unaffected by any gambling system applied to independent repetitions of the same game.

13

DISCONTINUITY AT
THE GOLDEN MEAN

(A paradox of proportional betting)

A paradox in mathematics is a result which contradicts what our intuition suggests should be true. Of course, to regard a finding as paradoxical is really to confess that our knowledge of the subject, our intuition, was less than perfect to begin with! Stanford Wong, in a paper presented to the Fifth National Gambling Conference, *What Proportional Betting Does to Win Rate,* suggested that proportional betting according to the Kelly Criterion might have a strange effect on conventional measures of win rate. Stewart Ethier recently published a paper in *The Journal of Applied Probability* entitled, "The Proportional Bettor's Return on Investment." Stewart's paper articulates, quantifies, and explains the phenomenon Wong's paper foreshadowed. In this issue of *C&S* I want to present another "paradox" of proportional betting, although not one involving win rate.

As background for this article it would be good to re-read my contribution to Volume 16 of *C&S* (see Chapter 8). In that issue I presented a method to calculate the chance that a gambler's fortune would be at an all time high. Assuming the gambler either won or lost a single unit at each play, it was shown that in the long run his chance of being at

(a) a brand new all time high was $2p - 1$
   and
(b) an all time high which had possibly been visited before was $2 - 1/p$.

The quantity p is the gambler's probability of winning an individual encounter and must be at least 1/2 for the formulas to make sense.

As an example, if the gambler could beat his adversary three times in five then p would equal .6. Substituting in expression (a) gives us $2(.6) - 1 = .2$, or 20% as the probability of our gambler's fortune being at a *brand new* all time high level. Expression (b) yields $2 - 1/.6 = .33$, or a 33% chance of being at an all time high. Note expression (b) is necessarily larger than (a) because it includes the 20% chance of being at a brand new all time high, just achieved, as well as a 13% chance of revisiting an all time high previously achieved.

What we want to do now is look into the effect of **proportional betting** on the gambler's chance of being at a brand new all time high. Before we do so, we ought to review the idea of proportional betting according to the Kelly Criterion. Let us assume, as before, that the gambler either wins or loses exactly what he wagers, with probability equal to p of winning and $1 - p$ of losing.

It has been shown that the gambler will optimize his long term capital growth rate and also have no risk of going broke if he varies his wagers depending upon the instantaneous value of his capital. In particular, the Kelly Criterion decrees wagering the fraction f = 2p − 1 of current capital on each coup. Using our previous example with p = .6, we conclude that the gambler will get filthy rich fastest by wagering 20% of what he possesses on each play.

Since the optimal Kelly betting fraction coincides with the gambler's long run probability of achieving a new all time high when flat betting one unit (*not* the Kelly Criterion), it would be interesting to know the gambler's chance of being at an all time high if he does wager according to the Kelly Criterion. The following table displays the empirical chance of being at an all time high during 1,000,000 trials for various values of the success probability p and betting fraction f = 2p − 1.

p	f	Chance of being at all time high
.505	.01	.0054
.55	.10	.0607
.60	.20	.1320
.70	.40	.2797
.80	.60	.5013
.90	.80	.6706

We note that with proportional betting the chance of an all time high is less than f = 2p − 1 but greater than half of f. To infer other values of the function which relates the probability of being at an all time high to the fraction f, we might be tempted to graph these six values and connect them with a smooth curve. Now, if I asked you to guess the chance of an all time high when f = .62 (p = .81) what would you respond?

Most reasonable interpolaters (those who infer unknown values from a restricted set of values in a table) would probably say "A little above .50, perhaps .51 or .52." Did you guess this? If so, don't congratulate yourself because you're way off! The correct answer is very close to .43! As a mathematician would say, the function relating the two quantities is not an increasing one.

Let's look into this a little more closely. Here are two more entries to append to our table of six figures:

p	f	Chance of all time high
.8085	.617	.5255
.8095	.619	.4286

What's this? A virtually infinitesimal increase of f from .617 to .619 occasions a *drop* of almost 10% in the chance of an all time high! How can this be?

It's time to observe that a loss in a particular play will change the gambler's fortune by a multiplicative factor of $(1 - f)$ and that a win will increase capital by the factor $(1 + f)$. To be at an all time high the gambler must necessarily have won his most recent game. If he had been at an all time high at the previous stage he would certainly arrive at a new all time high following a win. But he could also arrive at a new all time high if he had been just below a previous all time high and the factor of $(1 + f)$ was large enough to boost his current fortune sufficiently.

To take another perspective, suppose a gambler was at an all time high *two* games earlier. He then loses a game and wins a game. Could he have achieved a brand new all time high? The answer is no because the loss and subsequent win will have multiplied his previous all time high by the factor $(1 - f)(1 + f) = 1 - f^2$ which is *less* than one. Therefore his subsequent capital would be less than the previous all time high.

Now imagine the gambler who was at an all time high undergoes a sequence of three trials resulting in a loss followed by two wins. Would he arrive at a new all time high? The answer depends upon how big f is, for his multiplication of capital due to the three games will be $(1 - f)(1 + f)(1 + f)$. If we equate this multiplicative factor to one we will discover an interesting and critical value of f:

$$
\begin{aligned}
(1 - f)(1 + f)(1 + f) &= 1, \text{ or} \\
1 + f - f^2 - f^3 &= 1, \text{ from which} \\
f^3 + f^2 - f &= 0, \text{ or} \\
f^2 + f - 1 &= 0
\end{aligned}
$$

The final quadratic equation has only one (to us) meaningful solution, namely $f = (\sqrt{5} - 1)/2 = .618$. If the gambler is betting precisely this fraction, then a sequence of one loss and two wins will not change his capital at all. But, if the gambler bets any fraction less than $(\sqrt{5} - 1)/2$ then his capital will have grown to a new all time high and any fraction greater than $(\sqrt{5} - 1)/2$ will result in a decrease of capital. For instance if $f = .617$, then $(1 - f)(1 + f)(1 + f) = 1.0014$, while with $f = .619$, $(1 - f)(1 + f)(1 + f) = .9987$.

123

Evidently the sequence (Lose, Win, Win), occurring after a previous all time high has been achieved, is primarily responsible for the 10% *drop* in probability we observe when f is very close to $(\sqrt{5} - 1)/2$ (equivalently p is close to $(\sqrt{5} + 1)/4 = .8090$). If f is just a little below this value there is about a 53% chance of being at an all time high, but when f is just a bit above the critical value the probability of an all time high plummets to 43%.

In mathematics, a function whose graph can be drawn without picking the pencil up from the paper is called a continuous function. The graph relating the chance of an all time high to the fraction of capital bet is discontinuous because we have to pick up our pencil and reposition it about .10 units lower when passing through the value $f = (\sqrt{5} - 1)/2$:

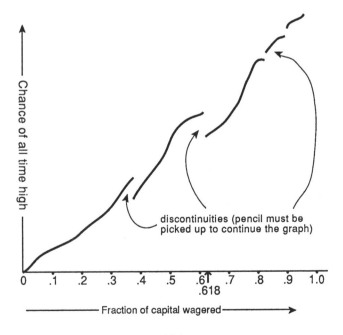

Chance of all time high

discontinuities (pencil must be
picked up to continue the graph)

| 0 | .1 | .2 | .3 | .4 | .5 | .6 | .7 | .8 | .9 | 1.0 |

.618

— Fraction of capital wagered —→

Actually the entire graph of the all time high function possesses an infinite number of these "discontinuities," little local drops in the generally increasing curve. Most of them are so small as to be imperceptible. We can discover two other large gaps in the graph by solving the equations

$$(1-f)^2(1+f)^3 = 1 \quad \text{and} \quad (1-f)(1+f)^3 = 1$$

for the values f = .38939 and f = .83929 respectively.

Sure enough, when we bracket these values of f with two nearby ones and simulate, we observe the phenomenon again:

p	f	Chance of all time high
.69469	.38938	.3003
.69470	.38940	.2659
.91964	.83928	.7385
.91965	.83930	.6807

Golden Mean

So why the title "Discontinuity at the Golden Mean"? Well, the value of $f = (\sqrt{5}-1)/2$, for which the most prominent of these breakdowns in the connectedness of the curve occurs, has a long and rich history in the development of mathematics. The ancient Greeks referred to it as the golden **mean**, or golden **ratio**, because they thought rectangles constructed with the ratio of sides .618 to one were the most aesthetically pleasing to behold. The shape was commonly used and strived for in the constructions of the time.

One very intriguing property of these rectangles is that if you cut off from the end a square, with side equal to the smaller dimension of the rectangle, what remains is another golden rectangle, similar in shape and with the same ratio of small to large side, .618 to one.

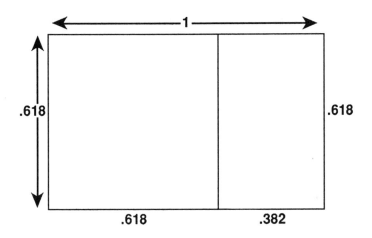

Observe that $\dfrac{.382}{.618} = .618$.

Another interesting occurrence of the golden mean is in the sequence of fractions 1/2, 2/3, 3/5, 5/8, 8/13, 13/21, 21/34, 34/55, etc. where each new numerator is the old denominator and each new denominator is the sum of the previous numerator and denominator. The numbers which appear, 1, 2, 3, 5, 8, 13, 21, 34, 55 etc. are called Fibonacci numbers after their Italian discoverer.

Observe the sequence of decimal equivalents striving mightily to approach the golden mean:

.5000, .6667, .6000, .6250, .6154, .6190, .6176, .6182.

The next one, 55/89, gives .6180 which is correct to four digits.

Betting systems based on the Fibonacci numbers possess many hitherto unexamined properties.

Two "Self-Styled Experts" - *Anthony Curtis and Peter Griffin at the Gambler's Book Club. Both were members of the ill-fated Karl's tournament team. (This chapter was originally published in article form in Arnold Snyder's* Blackjack Forum.*)*

14

SELF-STYLED EXPERTS
TAKE A BATH IN RENO

"Nice Guys Finish Last"
- Leo Durocher

The highlight of the 1986 Festival Reno was a city-wide blackjack tournament pitting twelve different casinos against each other. Each casino fielded a twelve man (correction: person) team. Every day, for three days, each player would play 52 hands at one of the casinos. Each casino would host twelve players for about one hour each day. Players were given $500 in non-negotiable chips at the beginning of each day's 52-hand round, regardless of what they finished the previous round with. Play took place with two rounds dealt per shuffle to four players at each of three tables.

Among the entrants was Karl's (Sparks) Hotel & Casino's dirty dozen - a collection of lockmasters, first-basers, rodmen, theoreticians, card counters, spooks, advisors, hole-carders, basic strategists, couponomists - you name it, every kind of degeneracy was represented. The theme of this assemblage was "the cream will rise to the top." Karl's finished last.

The prize structure of the tournament was such that all the entry fees would be returned to the players in prizes: $48,000 to the team finishing first and $24,000 to the runners-up. The winning team was the one with the greatest total cash out from the three days of play. The rules required a $10 minimum bet per hand with a $500 maximum. A team whose members all broke even at every session would have cashed out with 3 × 12 × $500 = $18,000 as a final total.

Karl's strategy going into the first round of play was to wager the table minimum on neutral or negative decks, 10% of bankroll on moderate advantages and 20% of bankroll on strong advantages. And with the choice of this strategy their fate was probably sealed!

The results of the first day's play were depressing indeed: Karl's had been unlucky, posting a total of $4600, well below the daily par of $6000. But more disturbing than this was the leading total: the Nugget had come in with almost $11,000! At Karl's strategy session the next morning their consulting theoretician advised, "Gentlemen, the Theory of Blackjack no longer applies." Little did they and their Strangeloveian hireling (three Heinekens an hour) realize it never had. It was decided not to panic, but to raise the previous day's 10% and 20% to 20% and 40%.

On Friday, Karl's scored another $4600, while the Nugget hit par, maintaining the lead with a second day total of $16,900, far in excess of Karl's $9300. The final day was marked by the tapping out of all twelve Karl's players, having committed themselves to Kamikaze tactics of each playing for a $10,000 table win. On the twelfth and final round, Karl's representative mercifully and fittingly went out on the first hand – 16 vs. 5 succumbing to the dealer's five card 17.

Surprisingly, the Nugget was overtaken on the final day by Western Village, the ultimate winner by $24,000 to $22,000, leaving Karl's worthies with nothing to show for their weekend but three monogrammed t-shirts and a hat. Had these "experts" been the victims of bad luck?

Well, yes and no. "Yes" in the sense that considering the cards dealt to them they wouldn't have won regardless of betting strategy. "No" in that the strategy adopted on the first day probably only had about a 2% chance of beating the *average best score* of the eleven other teams.

The crucial observation came from a bystander watching the carnage of Karl's suicidal charge halfway through the final day: "Betting the way you were, you didn't rate to win anyway." Thus spoke Robert Etter, up in Reno for a weekend bridge tournament and some desert stargazing with his telescope. Etter, not really from Georgia, although his undergraduate degree is from one of their diploma mills, observed intuitively that if there were many competing teams betting big, then Karl's team would have virtually no chance by betting small, regardless of their level of skill.

Post-tournament analysis confirms Etter's observation by showing that the winning final total of $24,000 was not at all improbable and, in fact, was just about the expected result. It is difficult to mathematize precisely the eleven competing teams' styles of play, but the assumption of a flat $150 bet with a 2% negative expectation per hand probably mimics well the drift (expectation) and volatility (standard deviation) of the typical opponent's play.

Under these assumptions, the expected final result for a team would be to lose 2% of their 1872 bets overall, namely to finish 37.4 big bets below par. The standard deviation for a team's play would be approximately $1.1 \times \sqrt{1872}$, or about 47.5 bets. Note that expectation is a constant $(-.02)$ times n, the number of hands, while standard deviation is another constant (1.1) times the square root of n. In the *very* long run $.02 \times$ n will dominate $1.1 \times \sqrt{n}$ but in the relatively short space of n = 1872 hands the standard deviation is the controlling factor.

To continue the analysis we dip into the theory of order statistics from a standard normal distribution, it being well known that the result of 1872 blackjack hands subject to a bounded bet is very nearly a Gaussian variable. Obscure sources reveal that the expected value of the largest of a sample of eleven normal variables (the competing, "inferior," teams) is to be *1.58* standard deviations above the mean. For our blackjack scenario, this translates into a final score of $-37.4 + 1.58\,(47.5) = +38$ big bets. In terms of the tournament, this would be $18,000 + 38\,(150) = $23,700$ as the typical result for the best of eleven teams.

Now, the questionable part of this analysis is the convenient assumption of a flat $150 bet. If, in fact, the *average* bet were $150 (experience at the table suggests this), then any deviation from flat betting of $150, but still averaging $150, would increase the fluctuation (standard deviation) of the team's bankroll. So, if the expected loss of 37.4 × $150 is correct, then the presumed standard deviation of 1.58 × 47.5 × $150 is too small; if the standard deviation is correct, then the expected loss is less than assumed. Conclusion: as long as the average bet is close to $150, the expected winning total of eleven teams would be about $24,000, as it was.

With a bet spread of $10 to $100 what chance would Karl's have to top $24,000? An overly optimistic analysis of their chances would restrict the discussion to the assumption of 468 large bets of $100, one for every other deck, on the average, with a presumed advantage of 2% on these wagers only. Assume the remaining 1404 small bets have no effect. Then Karl's would have an expected final total of 18,000 + .02 (46,800) = $18,936 with a standard deviation not much in excess of $1.1 \times \sqrt{468} \times 100 = \$2380$. Their chance of topping a typical best of $24,000 would be the area under the normal curve to the right of

$$\frac{24000 - 18936}{2380} = 2.13 \text{ standard deviations,}$$

which is less than 2%.

Moral? The casino blackjack player counts on very large n with a small constant of proportionality, the tournament player on the square root of relatively small n with a large multiplier.

15

MATHEMATICAL EXPECTATION FOR THE PUBLIC'S PLAY IN CASINO BLACKJACK

(The mathematical percentage for casino games (example: 1.4% for the line in craps, 5.3% for all but one obscure bet in roulette) is a matter of interest and, with the glaring exception of blackjack, public knowledge. This mathematical expectation is of importance to casino management because it can be used to project very accurately how much of the money placed on gambling tables the casino should, in the long run, earn.

The problem of measuring the effective mathematical percentage for blackjack bets, made by multitudes of players with freedom to play their cards as they wish and correspondingly different levels of skill, will be discussed. Extensive observations of the public's play in actual casino blackjack will be used to produce sharp estimates of the per capita rate of loss at casino blackjack. Despite the difficulty of measuring the rate of loss per dollar bet, rather than per individual player, informed conjecture on this alternative measure will also be presented.)

"Most people know in their minds what the right play is. It's just that sometimes their bodies won't let them do it".

- M. Sherman

I Introduction

For independent trials gambling games and, as a matter of practicality, also the game of baccarat, a casino's gross revenue for any given time period can be determined by simply recording the amount of money wagered on each of the available bets and multiplying by the associated and *known* mathematical expectations for these bets. As an example, if $380 is wagered in an hour at the roulette table, the casino is mathematically entitled to 2/38=5.26% of this, or $20. (We ignore one obscure and seldom made wager with house advantage 3/38=7.89%.) Good sources for these mathematical expectations are Epstein [2] and Wilson [5].

This sort of information can be useful to casino management in order to decide if it is economically feasible to keep a particular game operating. Merely monitor how much action there is over a period of time, determine the expected gross revenue, and compare this to the cost of operation and desired profit.

Unfortunately, that most popular and fascinating of games[1], blackjack, has proven an exception. One of the unique aspects of blackjack lies in the fact that players are given the choice not just of how much to bet, but also how to play after the wager is made. The many different choices exercised by the public (ways of playing

[1] I regard slot machines as an addiction rather than a game.

136

their cards) render impossible a precise determination of the casino's mathematical expectation in this game. A good account of the speculation that has occurred about this house advantage appears in Thorp [4]. "Dealer mimic" and "never bust" strategies were shown to give a house advantage between 5% and 6%, while recommended strategies of card experts at the time were rated at about 3%. With the discovery of the "basic strategy" (defined later) by Baldwin, Cantey, Maisel, and McDermott [1] and its subsequent publicity from Thorp's book in the mid sixties, the quality of the public's play undoubtedly underwent a quantum leap upwards, and presumably continues to improve today, although perhaps it is now approaching an asymptote.

The purpose of this paper is to present an efficient method of empirically determining any casino's mathematical expectation along with some tentative conclusions, based on extensive observation, of the current state of the casino's advantage over the blackjack playing public in the United States as of the Spring of 1987.

II Other Studies

I am aware of only two previous attempts at measuring the casino advantage in blackjack. The first was an unpublished study prepared for a Canadian government branch in the late '70s. Some 70,000 hands were observed in casinos, with a record kept of the amounts bet, won, and lost by the public. It resulted that the average loss of the public was 3.8% of what it had wagered.

The statistical significance of this figure is somewhat difficult to assess because the 70,000 bets were not identical. Had the wagers all been the same, the standard error of the 3.8% loss would have been $1.1/\sqrt{70,000} = .42\%$, where 1.1 is taken as the standard deviation of an individual blackjack hand played with Canadian rules. Under this assumption, a 95% confidence interval would have been 3.8% ±.8%. However, the varying size of the bets makes the actual precision of this estimate much poorer, although it is difficult to say how much wider the true confidence interval should have been.

The inefficiency of this approach will become evident later: had the 70,000 observations been conducted by the recommendations of this paper the standard error (assuming constant wagers) would have been .02% rather than .42%.

The second treatment of the problem was contained in two papers submitted to the Fifth National Conference on Gambling at Lake Tahoe in October of 1981 by ECON Inc., a New Jersey consulting firm. A consensus of guesses by casino employees about how often the "general public" would make various decisions at the blackjack table was used to postulate a strategy which was then simulated. ECON's designation "general public" deliberately excluded both basic strategists and card counters and further categorized the public into two groups labeled "novice" and "experienced". Anomalously, the "experienced" group was defined in such a way that it suffered by .03% from the introduction of the favorable early surrender rule, while the "novice" group gained .19%, thus rendering the dichotomy somewhat dubious.

In another part of their study ECON observed actual players wagering on some 250,000 black-jack hands. Had these quarter million observations been made by the methods of this paper, the public's expectation could have been estimated with a standard error of .01%.

III Basic Strategy, Definition and Implication for Casinos

"Basic strategy" is the set of decision rules, covering all possible choices a player might encounter, which maximizes his average gain, or expectation, playing one blackjack hand against a complete pack (or shoe) of cards. For subtle differences in rules and numbers of decks employed from casino to casino, there are equally minor modifications of this basic strategy. Its mathematical expectation too depends on these rules, varying in the major casinos of the United States from a .0% (Las Vegas Strip single deck) to a .9% (six decks, dealer hits soft 17, double down on ten and eleven only) advantage for the house. Typically a .5% player disadvantage may be considered representative, being very close to that appropriate for all of Atlantic City, multiple deck blackjack on the Las Vegas Strip, and the common single deck game in Northern Nevada.

The basic strategy and its measured player expectation are the result of absolutely precise probabilistic calculations and not subject to any sampling error whatsoever. They may be thought of as having been confirmed by a computer cycling through every single one of the billions of possible sequences of cards that could occur in a hand of blackjack.

139

If every player used the basic strategy, then casinos could not afford to deal the game, at least under their present rules. The .5% expected win for the casino would not be sufficient to pay the dealer, floor person, cocktail waitress, and other overhead expenses. It is only because of the public's ignorance of the basic strategy, or refusal to employ it, that the game of casino blackjack remains viable.

This latter observation contains the germ of the method used here to measure the public's (and consequently the house's) expectation at blackjack: rather than observing how much the public wins or loses, measure how much they deviate from this base line, known standard, the basic strategy. The actual monetary result of even a large sample of blackjack hands is subject to enormously large random fluctuations; the measured deviations from basic strategy, it turns out, are not.

IV How I Did It

The method of sampling used to quantify the public's performance is based on the observation of how people seated at actual casino blackjack tables really play their cards, rather than their, or someone else's, opinion on the matter as recorded in a survey. The variable measured will be the percentage cost of whatever deviations from basic strategy they employ. It will be designated by the letter E, to connote "error".

Before proceeding, it will be instructive to examine a hypothetical example. The "observer" (*sans* white lab coat and clip board, not wishing to draw attention to himself) sidles up behind seven players at a six deck game in Atlantic City. The dealer faces an ace and the seven players act as follows on their respective hands: ("T" stands for a generic ten-valued card.)

Player	Hand	Action	E(%)
# 1	(T5)	draw and bust	0
2	(99)	insure, split, stand on (97) and (93)	53
3	(TT)	insure, stand	4
4	(T9)	stand	0
5	(92)	draw, reach 17	0
6	(T7)	insure, draw once and reach 20	12
7	(96)	draw, reach 17	0

The observer, before recording the post-insurance actions of players #2 and #6, waits to see the dealer's down card. Had it been a ten for a dealer blackjack, players #2, #3, and #6 would have been assessed a 3.7% error only, for buying insurance (which is contrary to basic strategy even if it wins), but no further penalties since their subsequent actions would have been moot.

However, in this case imagine the down card is a three. The observer records player #2's erroneous split of (99) and stands on (97) and (93) and player #6's incorrect hit on (T7). He pays no attention to further activity at this table, being completely unconcerned with whether the dealer breaks or not or whatever money might change hands. The observer then slips unobtrusively to the next table to continue sampling or races back to his motel to gleefully look up the penalties for the players' mistakes.

Assuming the latter, here's how the E-values are arrived at. Players #1, #4, #5, and #7 played according to basic strategy and consequently are given scores of zero. Player #3 mistakenly insured, receiving a score of 3.7% (2 × 96/311 − 215/311 = 7.4% is divided by two since the insurance wager is for only half of the original wager), which is rounded to the nearest whole number, four. Player #2 is penalized (⁻9.31 − ⁻12.18) = 2.87(%) for splitting (99), (⁻35.43 − ⁻66.53) = 31.10(%) for standing on (93), (⁻51.36 − ⁻66.33) = 14.97(%) for stopping on (97), as well as the insurance 3.7% for a total score of 52.64, which is then rounded to 53. Player #6 has (⁻47.63 − ⁻55.70) = 8.07(%) added to his insurance penalty for a total of 11.77, which is then rounded off.[2]

Had this been the only data in the sample, it would have been summarized as follows: the public misplayed three hands out of seven (the multiplicity of mistakes of players #2 and #6 is ignored, although penalties are additive) with an average deviation from basic strategy of 69/7 = 9.86%. Since six deck basic strategy in Atlantic City is associated with a negative player expectation of .46%, these hypothetical players, while under observation (the seven hands), would be considered to have played at a 9.86 + .46 = 10.32% disadvantage.

Over 11,000 observations were made in just this fashion, in Reno, Lake Tahoe, Las Vegas, and Atlantic City, and the data will be displayed presently. In order to avoid monitoring certain players disproportionately often, the observer

---

[2] The precise figures quoted for splitting (99), standing on (97) and (93), and hitting (T7) come from an exact computer program. Reasonable approximations can be inferred from [3].

(namely me, the author!) would sample each playing spot twice during a particular time period. Thus during slack periods of the day the number of observations could be very small, occasionally fewer than twenty, while during the busy evening sessions when the casino was full, samples approaching 400 in size were not uncommon.

This technique in a sense stratified the sample correctly for the number of hands being played during different time periods of the day. Had a fixed number of observations been made at different times during the day, say 200, one would have risked the possibility of entering a virtually empty casino with perhaps one table, thus rendering the observer much more conspicuous and biasing the overall sample in the direction of these few players' levels of skill, whether it be high (close to basic strategy) or low (frequent and costly deviations from basic strategy).

Let us now, before considering and responding to possible objections to the sampling plan, turn to the results of this transcontinental blackjack investigation!

V How Well Does the Public Play Blackjack?

The public plays better than many astute pundits believe. Estimates given by casino-wise gambling pros ranged from 3% to 5%, some probably based on a hazy recollection of the figures given by Thorp for "dealer-mimic" or "never-bust" strategies and others on an attempt by casino personnel to extrapolate from the known hold percentages of blackjack and other games.

I myself had written [3] "the typical uninformed tourist probably gives the casino about 3% of his action". The basis for this conjecture was the assumption of a consistent, albeit uninformed, strategy of

(a) standing on 15 and above, hitting 14 and below regardless of the dealer's up card,
(b) always doubling 11, nothing else,
(c) standing on soft 17 and above ("like the dealer"), and
(d) splitting aces only, nothing else.

Experienced players should concede, upon reflection, that such a player is almost surely worse than *average*, although certainly not the worst player encountered. (The pathologies of very bad players tend to come to mind more easily due to the selectivity of memory.) At any rate, the strategy above can be shown to be 2.7% worse than basic strategy for Las Vegas Strip or Atlantic City blackjack.

Without further ado, here's what the numbers gathered between March and May of 1987 cause me to conclude:

1. The public misplays about one hand in six or seven (a typical mistake costing about 9% when it occurs) and is about 1.4% worse than basic strategy.

2. Atlantic City players are palpably and demonstrably better players (closer to basic strategy) than those in Nevada, by perhaps

1.1% to 1.5%.[3]

3. The standard deviation of the variable E, the public's measured error in basic strategy on an individual hand (recall E has the value 0 in about 85% of the cases, when basic strategy is followed), is between 4% and 5%, the former applying in Atlantic City, the latter in Nevada.

Here then, region by region and casino by casino, are the figures. A 95% confidence interval follows each regional mean. (n = number of hands, f = number of misplayed hands)

Casino	n	f	ΣE	ΣE^2	$\overline{E}$	s
Atlantic City						
A	764	101	899	16263	1.17	4.5
B	614	105	789	13536	1.29	4.5
C	491	81	544	6470	1.11	3.4
D	758	116	768	9059	1.01	3.3
E	608	75	516	6785	.84	3.3
F	1164	177	1455	22480	1.25	4.2
AC summary	4399	655	4971	74593	1.13(±.12)	4.0
Las Vegas						
G	799	123	1068	17478	1.34	4.5
H	1173	189	2062	43344	1.76	5.8
I	497	72	623	9597	1.25	4.2
J	184	25	229	3675	1.24	4.3
K	276	42	462	9950	1.67	5.9
L	136	25	273	4623	2.01	5.8
M	893	181	1906	35179	2.13	5.9
LV summary	3958	657	6623	123846	1.67(±.17)	5.3

[3] This was foreseen by Mike Moore, casino manager of the Four Queens, who said that the dealers in New Jersey practically could play the hands of the players without instruction, so accustomed were they to the uniformity of their play.

Reno

N	366	46	371	4400	1.01	3.4
O	1594	268	2611	42657	1.64	4.9
P	375	50	483	7380	1.29	4.2
Reno summary	2335	364	3465	54437	1.48(±.19)	4.6

Lake Tahoe

Q	45	7	84	1480	1.87	5.4
R	162	21	244	4693	1.51	5.2
S	67	8	45	339	.67	2.1
T	58	6	87	2027	1.50	5.7
LT summary	332	42	460	8539	1.39(±.54)	4.9

Reno/Tahoe	2667	406	3925	62976	1.47(±.18)	4.6
Nevada	6625	1063	10548	186822	1.59(±.12)	5.1
Grand Total	**11024**	**1718**	**15519**	**261415**	**1.41(±.10)**	**4.7**

The overall figure of 1.41% average deviation from basic strategy suggests that the typical blackjack player is probably losing just under 2% of his wager, assuming a .5% disadvantage for basic strategy. But, there is clear evidence that this figure does not apply homogeneously from coast to coast or from casino to casino.

It was obvious within 15 minutes of watching them that Atlantic City players were superior to their Nevada brethren. The sample means (1.13% and 1.59%) for these two locations differ by more than five standard deviations.

Within Nevada the sample means for Las Vegas and Northern Nevada (1.67% and 1.47%) are 1.6 standard deviations apart. The difference here, however, seems more likely to reflect the variation in rules between the two areas rather than a radically different level of knowledge. In Reno there are fewer strategic options available for doubling down, hence less opportunity to misplay the basic strategy.

Almost certainly there are differences in performance among some of the casinos in Las Vegas, although less obviously so in Atlantic City or Northern Nevada. The sample sizes are too small to support these, although it is interesting to speculate that the casinos with greater "walk in" traffic seem to have customers with a poorer grasp of basic strategy.[4] Surprisingly, the worst samples tended to appear in the late morning and early afternoon. Perhaps this could be attributed to an influx of freshly rested and breakfasted tourists busily losing their allotted $20 bill; by later in the day evolution has taken its course.

(After witnessing a surprisingly good performance of only seven inconsequential errors in 56 hands in what was clearly going to be the worst casino in the sample, I couldn't avoid thinking "Well, they're finally beginning to learn". When I returned a few hours later for another sample and picked up the action at the first table where

---

[4] This was suggested to me by Ken Adams, manager of the Comstock Casino in Reno.

the man on first base had just been dealt (A8), I mused "The beat goes on; he can't misplay this one!" As if sensing my satisfied presence behind him, he slowly pulled out extra money and doubled — against an ace! The other three players at the table proceeded to stand on 14's and 15's. Yes, the beat was going on.)

Without a doubt, the major problem area for the public is its failure to risk busting stiff hands against dealers' up cards of seven through ace; .5% of the total error rate of 1.4% comes from this source, much more than the .1% attributable to incorrectly drawing to stiffs against up cards of two through six. Indeed, the public's failure to double 10 and 11 when appropriate is, at .2%, more serious than risking busting against a small card. (I am reminded here of a dealer's admonition to a woman who had reluctantly decided to double down 11 against a six, finally saying "Oh well, I'll gamble", as she pushed out the extra chips: "Lady, if you don't double, then you *are* gambling!") Misplaying soft 17, incorrect pair splitting, and taking out insurance all measured about .1% each.

Although an exact account of the dealers' up cards was not kept for hands played according to basic strategy, a reasonable approximation to the public's conditional error rate for each dealer up card can be reconstructed by assuming that each denomination occurred 1/13 of the time. What results is this:

Basic Strategy Error Rate By Dealer's Up Card (%)

	A	2	3	4	5	6	7	8	9	T
New Jersey	2.1	1.1	1.1	.6	.7	.8	1.9	1.8	1.3	.8
Nevada	3.0	1.0	1.2	1.1	1.2	1.6	3.6	2.1	1.5	.9
Overall	2.6	1.0	1.2	.9	1.0	1.3	2.9	2.0	1.4	.9

The misplaying of stiffs against the ace, seven, and eight tends to be very costly, far more so than against the nine or ten, when it often doesn't matter very much whether one hits or stands. But the error rate against the ace is really even more alarming than it appears, since the players are protected from making non-insurance mistakes in the 31% of the cases when the dealer has blackjack.

One of the obvious reasons people are reluctant to draw to stiffs even when they know it's the right thing to do is that they're guaranteed to stay alive in the hand for a few more seconds — until the dealer turns up the down card — whereas busting results in immediate loss. The psychological basis for this behavior was discussed by Nick Bond in a 1974 paper in *Organizational Behavior & Human Performance*. (An interesting historical note: Bond, then a Psychology professor, was the one who alerted me, in 1970, to Epstein's *Theory of Gambling and Statistical Logic* as a potential text for the course I taught which ultimately kindled my interest in blackjack.)

149

Curiously, Atlantic City players were significantly poorer than Nevadans in one respect: they insured almost three times as frequently. Otherwise they never split tens (Nevadans did 16 times), nor were they responsible for the doubles of hard 12 (against 5 and 7) and 14 (against 9) which occurred in Las Vegas. Only one player hit hard 17 and nobody failed to split aces. The worst hand was a double split of (66) and subsequent stand on (T6) against a ten, a 63% error.

VI Possible Objections

I anticipate two principal objections to the technique of sampling and treatment of data. The first one that will occur is embodied in the question "But what about the effect of card counters correctly departing from basic strategy right in front of your very eyes?" Among the 11,000 players (actually hands) observed, it would be generous to admit that there were 100 such individuals operating. Since 80% of the observations were in multiple deck games, it would be generous again to grant that the card counters correctly deviated from basic strategy and were subsequently misclassified ten times. The hands they were misclassified on would tend to have been the common departure plays like 16 versus ten for which there is small penalty anyway. Again it would be generous to assume an average 5% erroneous penalty for these hypothetical ten departures. In addition it is unlikely that in the 100 imagined hands played that the card counters gained more than an average of .5% per hand played from strategy variation. Were this all true, the grand total error of 15519% would have to be reduced to about 15419%, resulting in a 1.40% rather than 1.41% error rate.

To ease any lingering torment caused by the specter of the sampled casinos being haunted by hordes of card counters, one could quote one sided confidence intervals. For example, we can say with 95% certainty that the public's true error rate does not exceed 1.49%, leaving unspecified a lower bound.

The second objection could be directed at the assumed independence of observations at the same table where possibly as many as seven players would be facing the same up card, against which as we have seen there are probably different error rates. Further, it cannot be denied that players are influenced by what other players at the table do. For example, if the first player stands with 15 against a seven, then it would appear mildly antisocial for the next person, possibly knowing better, to hit her 15. Interactions like this could, of course, gravitate in the other direction and improve the quality of play.

(It's worth recounting a couple of anecdotes to illustrate such influences. In one instance in Atlantic City, a player had already reached in his stack for extra money to correctly double hard ten against a two. But before it became his turn, the player to his right, after hesitation, whacked out his 14 with a ten. The potential doubler was furious — the nincompoop had not only taken "his ten", but also destroyed the natural order of the cards, all at one fell swoop. Hence the second player didn't double, drew a three, lost the undoubled bet, was proven correct, and thus felt reinforced in his gambling insights. Result? I booked *him* for a 19% error, although probably he knew the basic strategy better than the man fined 7% for hitting his 14.

In another case in Las Vegas, a player appeared about to double (55) against the dealer's five. He made no move to separate his cards. The dealer's "Splitting or doubling?", with emphasis on the "splitting", left the player confused. Finally he split, perhaps believing he had to. After all, "Split any Pair" is posted on the table and may appear to some as an injunction rather than a privilege, witness the man at Casino "M" who had separated two nines and matched his bet before the dealer had even turned over his up card, a ten.)

Clearly then there is some correlation of basic strategy errors at the same table, and this would result in slightly higher standard errors than those quoted. How much higher, I'm not sure. I doubt that it would be much greater than that caused by rounding observed errors to the nearest integral percent, although I'm hard put to rationalize this speculation.

VII Per Capita and Per Dollar Win Rates

It is important to realize that the empirical expectation of 1.41% for the entire sample is a "per capita" figure — the average deviation from basic strategy per person, but without any regard to how much money the individuals are wagering. As we shall see shortly, the effective "per dollar" deviation from basic strategy is probably well below 1%. The primary reason for this is that higher wagers tend to be associated with a better quality of play. A secondary influence on the overall per dollar expectation, partially a corollary to the previous remark, would be any deliberate raising of bets on favorable decks by skilled card counters.

A simple example should clarify the issue here. Suppose in a casino there are 100 three-dollar bettors and one three-hundred-dollar bettor, all monitored once. The three dollar bettors have an average error rate of 2% and hence a total of 200% worth of errors. Imagine that the big bettor plays his one hand according to basic strategy. Then the per capita error rate will be $200\%/101 = 1.98\%$. However, the effective per *dollar* error rate will be a weighted average, $(300 \times 2\% + 300 \times 0\%)/600 = 1.00\%$, roughly half of the per capita rate.

The original intent for this study was to produce both of these error rates. After the first 1000 observations, the per capita error rate was 1.5% while the per dollar rate was 1%, approximately $300 in mistakes divided by $30,000 in action. This refined sampling, wherein not only were errors recorded but also every single player's wager, was then abandoned, for two reasons:

(1) It proved quite time consuming and also made the observer too conspicuous. Players became

aware of the observation and were bothered, among other things, by the idea that their wins and losses were being recorded, although this was not the case.

(2) It was evident that any confidence interval for the average wager would be very unstable indeed. Since essentially this quantity appears in the denominator, the per dollar win rate itself would be very unreliable given the number of observations feasible in the study. The presence or absence of just one big bettor at any given time would result in an enormous bias toward or away from his own caliber of play.

To confirm the intuition that big bettors were generally better educated players than the table-minimum fleas, a separate sample was kept (for the rest of the project) of the performance of players who wagered at least $100. It must be emphasized that no special effort was made to locate $100 bettors, but rather, their random appearances were noted for inclusion in a subsample from the overall study. The following statistics, already a part of the entire sample in section V, describe their performance.

n	f	ΣE	ΣE^2	$\bar{E}$	s
292	23	137	1271	.47($\pm$.23)	2.0

Clearly this group is better than the rest of the public of which it makes up only a small part per capita (somewhat less than 3%) but probably a significant part per dollar (conceivably 50%). It is also likely that $50 and $75 bettors are a-bove average, although perhaps not by as much as this group.

One difficulty in adjusting an individual casino's per capita error rate to a per dollar one is that there are very different wagering patterns from casino to casino and from season to season. While some rarely see any $100 bets, a casino like Caesars Palace may have as many as 28 hundred-dollar minimum tables operating at one time during a big fight promotion.

Regardless, if one wishes to measure the per dollar win rate, it would still be more efficient to associate the different wagers with the basic strategy errors (as in the first 1000 observations of this study) rather than to keep track of the amount of money actually won or lost. In this fashion, the ratio of the standard deviations for the numerators of the per dollar error rates would be at least $115/5=23$ (taking 115% as the stan-dard deviation of a blackjack result and 5% as a worst case standard deviation for the public's errors from basic strategy, regardless of wager-ing level). Hence a sample at least $23^2 = 529$ times as large of actual blackjack results would be required for the same precision attainable by the methods of this study.

This 500-fold reduction in sample size to achieve equal precision is what recommends the methods of this paper.

ACKNOWLEDGMENTS

1. All statistical calculations for this paper were done on a McDougall-Griffin 1937 computer.

2. I thank Mr. Tony Alamo of the Desert Inn in Las Vegas and Mr. Ken Adams of the Comstock Hotel & Casino in Reno for assistance in this project.

REFERENCES

1. Baldwin, Cantey, Maisel, and McDermott. *Journal of the American Statistical Association* 51 (1956): 419-439.

2. Epstein, R. A. *Theory of Gambling and Statistical Logic*. Rev. ed. New York: Academic Press,1977.

3. Griffin, P. A. *The Theory of Blackjack*. 3d ed. Las Vegas: Huntington Press, 1988.

4. Thorp, E. O. *Beat the Dealer*. New York: Vintage Books, 1966.

5. Wilson, A. *The Casino Gambler's Guide*. New York: Harper & Row, 1965.

16

EXTRA STUFF

****

Peter Griffin's Blackjack Quiz

1. Suppose you have a total of twenty. What dealer up card would you most like to see?

2. You're playing single deck blackjack in a casino allowing surrender. Alone at the table, you play two hands off the top of the deck. You're dealt a pair of sevens on each hand and the dealer's up card is a ten. How do you, as an expert, play the hands?

3. Why are short people more knowledgeable players than tall people?

4. The remaining 22 cards consist of 12 tens; two aces, sevens, eights, and nines; and one each, two and three. Estimate the advantage for optimal play with and without surrender.

5. Conventional blackjack rules, player has a pair of eights and dealer has a pair of nines (known to the player). Which side would you rather have, player or dealer?

157

Answers

1. An eight as dealer up card maximizes the player's expectation when he has a total of twenty. The dealer's frequent "pat" hands, with which he cannot draw, can neither beat nor tie the player. This also applies to a seven, but then the dealer draws more often, with the possibility of tying or beating the player. There are certain multiple card twenties, like (4, 4, 4, 4, 2, 2) with which the player has a better expectation against a seven than an eight, but they are rare and wouldn't occur with a correct drawing strategy.

2. You surrender your right hand (the first one you look at) and stand on the left (second) one! Remember, you won't know what's in the left one until you've resolved the right one. It's well known that (7, 7) is a basic strategy surrender against a ten because the expectation is −.5097, which is worse than a 50% loss. But, the removal of the right hand's two sevens raises the dealer's chance of busting to .2591 and hence the expectation by standing becomes .2591 − (1−.2591) = −.4818 for the left hand, better than a 50% loss.

3. There are two reasons. The first is that short people are more likely to glimpse the hole card when the dealer slides it underneath. The second reason is that John Luckman keeps Peter Griffin's *The Theory of Blackjack* on the very bottom shelf of the display counter at Gambler's Book Club where only dwarfs will see it.

4. This subset occurred during one of my practice sessions and the question of what it was worth so intrigued me that I ran all possible hands through the computer. My original guess of about 20% was far too low: the player's optimal strategy expectation is 32.1% without surrender and 35.8% with surrender. Resplitting of up to four tens was allowed. The basic strategy expectation is less than 6%.

5. The answer here depends upon the number of decks. I assume the player will resplit all eights and always hit 17 since he knows the dealer is pat with 18. In single deck the eight splitter has the best of it with an expectation of +2.69%, but in four decks the proposition turns sour for the player with a splitting expectation of –.20%.

John Luckman - *Founder of Gambler's Book Club. Mentor to many.*

****

A Typical Book Review

The authors join a growing host of individuals who seek to memorialize and celebrate their newly emerging understanding of the game of blackjack by writing books or articles about the subject. Thus the cluttering of an already overcrowded body of writing becomes compounded.

In the opening pages they inveigh that most blackjack books are paraphrases of Ed Thorp's *Beat the Dealer*. They then proceed to illustrate the point very well in the next hundred pages. As an example, their coining of the terms "actual count" and "computed count" for what other writers have settled on as "running count" and "true count" is a disingenuous and transparent attempt to appear to be presenting something new.

If this book were priced at $5 it could be recommended as diversionary reading; as the wine snobs say "you will be amused by its pretension." But the preposterously exorbitant price tag of $95 is just too big a joke. Serious novitiates in the art of card counting will be well advised to pony up less than one fifth of this price tag for the much more reliable guides of Wong, Thorp, Uston, Braun, Snyder or Humble. In fact for the price being asked, you could buy all of them; it just doesn't equate.

While my review may seem to be unduly negative, I do not mean to single out these authors from the multitude. The criticism I level I would apply to some extent to almost every book on blackjack since Thorp's *Beat the Dealer*.

****

Griffin Comments on 8–Spot Keno Ticket Story

2 March 84

Letters to the Editor
Hollywood, California

Dear Sir:

In the March issue, the redoubtable B.S. suggests the gambler who desires to turn $1 into $50,000 is better off to play an 8-spot keno ticket than to parlay his money at a crap table with a $2,000 limit. He states this latter activity has odds against it of "approximately a million to one." B.S. is wrong.

The chance of hitting an 8-spot is one out of 230,115, whereas the craps parlayer ("don't pass") has better than one chance in 85,471 of turning $1 into $50,000.

The craps bettor would have to win eleven bets in a row to raise his capital to the $2,000 limit. The chance of this is $(949/1925)^{11} = .000418$. Then he would bet in units of 2,000 until he achieved 50,000, or 25 new units. The chance of this is $(27/949)/((976/949)^{25} - 1) = .0280$. Multiplying gives .0000117. Actually, the craps parlayer can do a little better since, if he wins his first six bets to achieve $64, he would then only

161

bet $63 rather than the whole $64, as his specific parlay goal is $2,000 rather than $2,048. Extra dollars saved in this fashion might enable him to start over.

Please send, as a reward for catching B.S. in another mistake, $100,000,000 to:

Peter A. Griffin
Professor of Mathematics

(Stewart Ethier has since pointed out to me that the absolutely optimal chance of turning $1 into $50,000 is achieved by betting as much money as possible until one is closer than $2,000 to the $50,000 goal, at which time one bets exactly enough to hit $50,000 on the nose. For this strategy I have calculated that the bettor's chance of making it to $50,000 is one out of 83,565.)

The reference to the $100,000,000 is to a previous article written by B.S. in which he promised to give $10,000 to charity if anyone could find an error in it. I wrote the editor about that one, too. Needless to say, they printed neither letter, as their publisher had a strict editorial policy proscribing the appearance of my name, Stanford Wong's name, and, later, Stewart Ethier's name. Stewart and I managed to put one over on them, as the following letter they did print shows.

****

Guru Goof?

"Craps Guru" N.B. Winkless, Jr. made a serious error in the May issue. Ed Dratwa raised the

162

question of whether most shooters are out in seven rolls or less, and NBW replied, "No. The average number of rolls is between eight and nine." He should have answered, "Yes. In fact most shooters are out in six rolls or less."

It seems that NBW confused the mean and median in responding as he did. For the record, the probability of sevening out in six rolls or less is 0.502789 (rounded off to the nearest millionth).

Peter Stewart
Las Vegas, Nev.

Craps Guru Winkless: I wish I could get as much fun out of differentiating among mean, median and average as some of you educated guys do. All I know is that probability says a shooter can expect to roll 'em eight or nine times before his hand becomes history.

If I'm confused, I fear that sets no precedent.

****

Stewart's banishment from the pages of the magazine occurred shortly before this, when he raised objection to what seemed at the time an incredibly improbable parlay. In May of 1985 he submitted a manuscript to them entitled, "So You Think You Know Craps," consisting of twelve challenging probability questions related to the popular dice game. Receipt of his article was never acknowledged, and Stewart was highly surprised to see, a few months later, one of his questions appearing in their magazine as the basis of an article by their own "craps guru".

In order that Stew's intriguing questions may finally see the light of day we present them here, with his permission. Although I solved most of them once, in many cases I can no longer recall how! So, send your solutions to numbers 4-12 to Stewart.

S.N. Ethier
Department of Mathematics
University of Utah
Salt Lake City, Utah 84112

****

So You Think You Know Craps
by S. N. Ethier

You've played the game for years, and you've read several books on the subject, including perhaps *Scarne on Dice*. If anyone knows craps, you do. Right?

Not necessarily. Most (maybe all) books on craps contain the same information: the rules, the house advantages associated with the various bets, and a few words of advice. If that were the extent of your knowledge of blackjack, would you consider yourself a blackjack expert? Of course not.

So to determine who the real experts at craps are, we offer the following quiz. Begin by attempting to solve the first three problems. The correct solutions appear elsewhere in this issue. If you can correctly solve *at most one* of the three, stop. Sorry, but you are not an expert at craps.

164

If you can correctly solve at least two of the first three problems, try your luck on problems 4–12.

Craps Quiz

1. (EASY) Everyone knows that by taking or laying the odds, one reduces the casino's advantage. In a single-odds casino, what is the minimal house advantage at craps? (By definition, the house advantage is the ratio of the gambler's expected loss to his expected amount of "action." Except in the case of a tie, which results in no action, the amount of action is the amount bet.) Choose from among the following answers, expressed as percentages and rounded to the nearest thousandth. (a) 1.414 (b) 1.403 (c) .848 (d) .832 (e) .734 (f) .691 (g) .606 (h) .591 (i) .572 (j) .459 (k) .434 (l) other.

2. (EASY) If you bet one unit on each number of a 38-number roulette wheel simultaneously, you lose two units no matter what happens. Is there a combination of craps bets (found on standard layouts and made simultaneously) that loses at least one unit no matter what happens?

3. (EASY) What is the average length of a shooter's hand? That is, what is the average number of rolls needed to miss a point (A two, three, or 12 on a come-out roll does not end the shooter's hand.)

4. (MODERATE) You bet on the pass line or on come on two successive rolls of the dice. Given that you eventually win the first bet, what is

the (conditional) probability that you eventually win the second bet? In particular, is it greater than, less than, or equal to the (unconditional) probability 244/495?

5. (MODERATE) You bet on don't pass or don't come on every roll of the dice and lay full odds. When all six point numbers (4,5,6,8, 9,10) occur (at least once) without an intervening seven, the next seven has been compared to a grand slam home run. What are the odds against achieving all six point numbers (at least once) before a seven occurs?

6. (MODERATE) You make a place bet on six after the come-out roll. What is the average number of rolls needed to resolve this bet, keeping in mind that place bets are "off" on come-out rolls? Does it matter what the point was?

7. (HARD) You bet one unit on the pass line or on come on every roll of the dice. Consider your (conditional) expected win on the nth bet, given that you (eventually) lose the first $n - 1$ bets. Show that this tends to a positive limit as n tends to infinity and find it. What is the smallest n for which it is positive?

8. (HARD) On every come-out roll, player A bets one unit on the pass line, player B makes a one-unit place bet on six that pays seven to six, and player C makes a one-unit one-roll bet on 11 that pays 16 to one (British rules). No player bets on point rolls. If each player makes n bets, which one has the best chance of ending up a winner? Show that if n is sufficiently large, the answer does not depend on n. How large is "sufficiently large"?

9. (HARD) You bet one unit on the pass line or on come on every roll of the dice. Show that the probability that your actual winnings after n bets exceed your expected winnings by at least the square root of n units approaches a limit as n tends to infinity and find it.

10. (UNSOLVED) If you bet one unit on each of 35 numbers on a 38-number roulette wheel, you end up winning with probability 35/38. What combination of craps bets (made simultaneously) maximizes your chance of winning? (Proposition bets not found on standard layouts are disallowed.)

11. (UNSOLVED) Show that the expected number of unresolved pass line and come points after n rolls approaches a limit as n tends to infinity and find it.

12. (UNSOLVED) You have 100 units at a double-odds craps table and wish to double it before losing it. What should your first bet be to maximize your chance of success? (Bets must be in multiples of one unit.) Same question at a single-odds table.

For simplicity, assume in problems 4,7,9, and 11 that unresolved come bets are not "off" on come-out rolls.

Solutions to Problems 1 – 3

1. The correct answer is (h) .591. This can be achieved by betting three units on don't pass and laying the odds for six units, regardless of the point. This is known as maximizing full odds, and is permitted in virtually all single-

odds casinos. (See Friedman's *Casino Games* for details.)

2. Here is one possible solution. Bet 35 units on the pass line, 35 units on don't pass, and one unit on the one-roll bet that the barred number (2 or 12) will appear.

3. To solve this one, we need to know that if an experiment that results in "success" with probability p is repeated indefinitely, then the average number of trials needed to achieve the first success is $1/p$. Let p_i denote the probability of rolling a total of i.

First, the average number of rolls needed for a pass line decision can be computed as follows. If a natural or craps occurs on the come-out roll, only one roll is needed. If point i occurs, then $1 + 1/(p_i + p_7)$ rolls are needed on average. Weighting these results according to their probabilities gives 557/165, or about 3.376. This result was first published in the *American Mathematical Monthly* in 1909.

Next, the average number of pass line decisions needed for a miss-out is $1/(1 - p_2 - p_3 - p_{12} - 244/495) = 495/196$, or about 2.2526. Multiplying these two results together, we get the desired answer: 1671/196, or about 8.526.

****

My own difficulties with this now defunct magazine began in 1980 when I received a lengthy letter from the publisher informing me of his "intention to review your book . . . I can tell you in advance that you will not like the review . . . it (my book) is a cruel hoax perpetrated upon an unsuspecting public." The review was entitled, "The Good, The Bad and the Ugly," being actually a review of three books, of which mine was, needless to say, the last. This was the last time, to my knowledge, my name appeared in their pages.

****

April 1, 1983, Las Vegas

Peter Griffin, former columnist for this magazine, plunged to his death from the top story of the Gambler's Book Club. Griffin had become despondent recently about not being able to think of anything to write about.

His nondescript career as a writer about gambling topics was the result of an unfortunate accident, his selection by a group of students to conduct a course for them in the subject. This led to his first publication, a chapter in *Gambling and Society*, in which he developed a formula for variance when sampling is without replacement. It was not until several years later that he realized that this was a commonplace of existing statistical literature.

Sporadic contributions to the first six gambling conferences required him to learn computer programming. One of his innovative subroutines, the Fortran statement "727 go to 727," occasioned much attention from the computer operators. He was, until John Gwynn's advent into gambling research, the heaviest user on campus.

Griffin's first and only book, *The Theory of Blackjack*, was correctly panned by astute critics as "a cruel hoax" perpetrated by him and his publisher, Walter I. Nolan, "in an attempt to mislead the public." Needless to say, it was a commercial flop from which he hardly realized the price of a six pack of Heineken.

His sordid life closed amid accusations that he had plagiarized from one of Russell Baker's columns which began "Russell Baker, popular humorist for this newspaper jumped to his death from the ninth floor of the Times building today, because he couldn't think of anything to write about..."

He went to his grave without revealing what he claimed was his discovery of the maximal number of blackjack decks for which composition dependent basic strategy differed from infinite deck strategy. He is survived by two dogs, Pele and Paula.

Index

A

Academic Press   156
Adams, Ken   147, 156
Alamo, Tony   156
Albertan Gaming Control Board   102
American Mathematical Monthly   168
American Mathematical Society   100
Atlantic City   *(see also - New Jersey)*
        15, 43, 139, 141, 142, 144-147, 150, 151
Atlantic City Resorts Association   113
average result   6

B

baccarat   56, 110-111, 136
Baker, Russell   170
Baldwin, Cantey, Maisel, and McDermott   137, 156
Barney's Casino   99
basic strategy   13, 111-113, 137, 139-150, 152-153,
        155, 158, 159, 170
Beat the Dealer (see also - Thorp, Edward)   156, 160, 161
Bill's Casino   99
blackjack   13-16, 68, 73, 77, 90, 91, 110, 111-114, 129,
        130, 132-133, 135-156, 157-161, 164, 170
Blackjack Forum   128
Bond, Nick
        Organizational Behavior & Human Performance   149

Braun, Julian   160
Buffon, Count
  needle problem   94

C

Caesars Palace   155
Caesars Tahoe   111
Canadian rules blackjack   138
card counting   14-15, 106, 111, 113-114, 138, 150-
  151, 153, 160
Cardano   19
Casino & Sports (C&S)   12, 13, 27, 28, 38, 69, 104,
  110, 119
Chambliss, Carlton   111, 112, 113
  Playing Blackjack in Atlantic City   111
Christopher, John
  *On the Asymptotic Density of Some k-dimensional
    Sets*   98
Comstock Casino   147, 156
Cover, Tom   100
craps   1-11, 50, 52-53, 56, 63, 64, 76, 108, 110-111,
  115-116, 135, 161-168
  odds bet   77, 165, 166, 167
Curtis, Anthony   128

D

Desert Inn   156
drop   108, 109
Durocher, Leo   129

E

Eadington, William   99
early surrender   16, 113, 114, 138
ECON   106, 113, 114, 138, 139
Epstein, Richard A.   7, 8, 10, 136, 149, 156
  Theory of Gambling & Statistical Logic   7, 149, 156
Ethier, Stewart   76, 77, 111, 119, 162-164
  On the House Advantage   111
  The Proportional Bettor's Return on Investment   119

172

So You Think You Know Craps? 164
Etter, Robert 131
expectation 1, 2, 6, 8, 11, 13, 48, 49, 53, 55-56, 67, 73-74, 86, 90, 91, 132, 135-137, 139-140, 158

F

Fibonacci numbers 126, 127
Four Queens 145
Friedman, Bill
    Casino Games 168
Friedman, Joel
    Understanding and Applying the Kelly Criterion 85

G

Gambler's Book Club 12, 13, 128, 158, 160, 169
gambler's ruin 68, 69-82
Gambler's Rule of Thumb 19, 21, 22, 25, 27, 29
Gambling and Risk Taking, Fifth National Conference 85, 99, 111, 114, 119, 138
Gambling and Society 169
Gauss-Seidel Iteration 80, 82
Gwynn, John 169

H

Harper & Row 156
HIGH ROLLER 85, 86, 87, 88, 89
hold 107, 108, 109, 110
Housman, A.E. 85
Humble, Lance 160
Huntington Press 13, 156

I

independent trials 2, 7, 86, 136
infinite deck 14
insurance 141, 142, 148, 149
irrational numbers 96, 97

173

J

The Journal of Applied Probability 119
Journal of Operations Research 77
Journal of the American Statistical Association 156

K

Karl's Casino 128, 129, 130, 131, 133
Kelly Criterion 85-86, 90, 119-121
Keno 161-162

L

Lake Tahoe *(see also - Nevada ; Northern Nevada)* 1, 99,
    138, 142, 146
Las Vegas *(see also - Nevada)* 11, 13, 14, 53, 55,
    110, 112, 139, 142, 144, 145, 147, 150, 152,
    156, 163, 169
Law of Large Numbers 50, 63, 65
Leibnitz 2
Luckman, John 158, 159

M

martingale 115, 116
de Mere, Chevalier 19
Michigan State University 111
Moore, Mike 145
Monte Carlo Casino 100

N

negative expectation 2, 6, 11, 132, 142
Nevada 16, 144, 145, 146, 147, 149, 150
New Jersey 16, 113, 138, 145, 149
New Jersey Casino Control Commission 106
New Jersey Gaming Control Commission 113
Nolan, Walter I. 170
Northern Nevada 139, 147
Nugget, John Ascuaga's Casino 130, 131

P

Professional Blackjack (see also - Wong, Stanford) 59
proportional betting *(see also - Kelly Criterion)*
    85, 119, 120, 121

R

random walk   56, 59-64
rational number   94
relatively prime numbers   92, 97, 98
Reno *(see also - Nevada ; Northern Nevada)*   129, 131,
    142, 146, 147, 156
Reno, University of Nevada at   86, 111
Roginski, Tom   111, 112, 113
    Playing Blackjack in Atlantic City   111
roulette   25, 28, 30, 33, 49-56, 63, 64, 67, 68, 73-76,
    107-109, 135, 136, 165, 167

S

Scarne on Dice   164
Schwartz, Howard   12
Sherman, Michael   136
Silver Slipper   2
simultaneous wagers   85-91
slot machines   136
Snyder, Arnold   128, 160
Sparks   129
standard deviation   51-52, 54, 132-133
standard score   52
Stewart, Peter   163
surrender (late)   157, 158, 159

T

The Theory of Blackjack   13, 50, 77, 130, 156, 158, 170
*Theory of Gambling and Statistical Logic (see also - Epstein,
    Richard A.)*   7, 149, 156
Thorp, Edward   98, 99, 101, 137, 143, 156, 160, 161
    Beat the Dealer   156, 160, 161
ties, treatment of   110-111

transcendental numbers   91, 96, 100

U

U.S. Playing Card Co.   100
Unit Normal Linear Loss Integral (UNLLI)   51, 52
Uston, Ken   113, 114, 160
Utah, University of   111, 164

V

variance   51, 53, 91, 169
Vintage Books   156

W

Western Village Casino   131
Wilson, Allan   73, 136, 156
    Casino Gambler's Guide   73, 156
Winkless, N.B. Jr.   162
Wong, Stanford   98, 99, 101, 119, 160, 162
    Professional Blackjack   59
    What Proportional Betting Does to Win Rate   119